Praise for *My Animal, My Self*

"*My Animal, My Self* is a must-read for everyone who has animals in their lives. Marta Williams clearly explains the important concept of mirroring between animals and their people; her engaging style and heartwarming stories can help everyone understand how to benefit from this wonderful gift our animals have to give us."
— Carol Gurney, founder of the Gurney Institute of Animal Communication and author of *The Language of Animals*

"Marta Williams has created a book with thought-provoking elements that combine both scientific intelligence and deeper intuitive perspectives that offer us unique ways of thinking and great solutions. The valuable exercises included here give us the opportunity to improve our lives with a deeper and broader understanding of who we are, how we are operating, and how we can make changes for the benefit of ourselves and our animals, based on the truth and reality of our connections to them. The collection of wonderful, worldwide case histories provides solid confirmation of these ideas. I feel honored to have been included in this stunning gift to all of us on the planet. Thank you, Marta Williams!"
— Tina Hutton, creator of Alternative Methods in Horsemanship and Finding Your Rider Within; TTEAM/TTouch Practitioner, Level 3; and MBS Feldenkrais Master Practitioner

"Our understanding of the animals in our lives is finally evolving from a need to dominate and control them to a sense of the deep connection we share with them. Marta Williams brings this connection into focus by showing how we and our animals mirror each other, picking up each other's inner world and reflecting it back, giving us insight and healing. *My Animal, My Self* is essential for those of us who want to understand the profound relationship between our animals and ourselves. This is a groundbreaking, enlightening book."

— Margot Lasher, author of *And the Animals Will Teach You*

"Marta Williams breaks new ground by presenting unexplored aspects of animals as mirrors to human qualities and frailties. She uses an intriguing variety of practical examples, exercises, and a mirroring questionnaire that will have readers recalling and relating to animals, past and present, in an entirely new way. *My Animal, My Self* shows us how to go beyond training and 'fixing' animals to changing the images of ourselves reflected by their honesty, love, and compassion. This is a book we will heartily recommend to everyone who has chosen and been chosen by an animal. Now they will understand the expanded and true significance of those choices. What a gem of a book."

— Allen and Linda Anderson, authors of
Angel Dogs, Angel Cats, and *Angel Horses*

"This book is an extraordinary gift to each of its readers and to the animals who love us. The perceptions and feelings revealed in these pages are presented with clarity and vulnerability as the author honestly shares not only her own heartfelt experiences but also those of colleagues, friends, and students who have had the grace to step forward and honor the profound wisdom of their animals. If my own experience is any indication, tears of the private kind we only share with the animals we love will be shed in different moments by every reader of this book."

— Rick Davis, director and producer of
That's My Baby and *Adoption Tales* for Animal Planet

My Animal,
My Self

Also by Marta Williams

Ask Your Animal
Beyond Words
Learning Their Language

My Animal, My Self

A Breakthrough Way to Understand
How You and Your Animal
Reflect Each Other

Marta Williams

New World Library
Novato, California

New World Library
14 Pamaron Way
Novato, California 94949

The material in this book is intended for educational purposes only. No expressed or implied guarantee of the effects of the use of the recommendations
can be given or liability taken.

Flower essence remedy descriptions used with permission of Bram Zaalberg,
www.bloesem-remedies.com.

Text design by Tona Pearce Myers

Library of Congress Cataloging-in-Publication Data is available.

First printing, June 2013
ISBN 978-1-60868-169-3
Printed in the USA on 100% postconsumer-waste recycled paper

 New World Library is proud to be a Gold Certified Environmentally
Responsible Publisher. Publisher certification awarded by Green Press
Initiative. www.greenpressinitiative.org

10 9 8 7 6 5 4 3 2 1

*To the animals in our lives who have taught us, helped us heal,
and shown us a love that knows no limit*

Contents

Acknowledgments

N o book is an island; many people contribute to the creation of
any book, even if they are just the inspiration for it. In the case
of *My Animal, My Self,* this book would not be before you without
the input of a good number of animals as well. My thanks to everyone, animals included, who lent their stories for you to read and to
all those who helped make this book a reality — most especially to
Gerrie Huijts from the Netherlands, who kept asking me, "When
are you doing the book on mirroring? When will it be coming out?"
If she hadn't kept asking, I might not have pursued it so doggedly. I
must also thank Monique Muhlenkamp of New World Library for
encouraging me to repitch the book to my editor, Georgia Hughes.
The second time was the charm. Thank you, Georgia, for taking a
chance on such an unexplored topic and for your skillful editing.

Thanks to the many professionals who lent their time and
expertise to this work, including psychologists Margot Lasher,
Dickelle Fonda, Jay Rice, and Marie-José Hakens; holistic veterinarians Dr. Marty Goldstein and Dr. Lisa Pesch; horse expert Tina
Hutton; horse-assisted learning practitioner Dr. Beverley Kane;
animal communicator Carol Gurney; human/animal chiropractor

Dr. Maryanne Kraft; Lily Peters, who translated portions of Bram Zaalberg's book; and Bram Zaalberg, the Dutch flower essence creator, who allowed me to design an exercise for people and their animals based on his material and sent me the translation of his Dutch flower remedy guide and his mirroring exercise — for balancing your inner self — to share with you.

Introduction

When I was just starting out in the world of living with dogs, I took my seven-month-old female puppy named Brydie, who was part Border collie, part Dalmatian mix — a combination I now know was just asking for trouble — to a beginning dog-obedience class. The class was held outside in a weed-strewn, concrete lot in the middle of the small town where I lived. The woman who taught the class was one of those classic dog people — whistle around her neck, leathery skin, hair bleached and dried to straw by the sun and wind. Pretty much within the first five minutes of class, Brydie and I had a training-crisis meltdown. I had Brydie on a leash, and a woman in the class came up to us with her dog to visit. My erstwhile sweet and loving baby girl turned into The Alien: huge fangs appeared out of nowhere, a hideous scream issued from the depth of her chest, and she lunged with full force at the woman's dog. For the record, I can't recall anything about the woman or her dog, though I'm sure I would have remembered if her dog had been in any way aggressive. I have so little recall because I was in a complete state of shock. What I do remember is hearing the thin, cheery, Barbara Woodhouse–like voice of the trainer calling out something like,

Marta and Brydie

"Oh, don't worry — that's perfectly normal." I was incredulous at the idea that this behavior was normal. Then as I stood there non-plussed, Brydie did it again: lunged with all her weight, saliva flying and eyes ablaze. I thought to myself, "If this is normal, I want nothing to do with it." I was so freaked out I just left the class. Today, I couldn't tell you if the trainer tried to stop me or reason with me or even if I got my money back. I was in deep distress.

I had adopted Brydie from the shelter just three months earlier, and I had already somewhat realized that I was now the owner of a whirling dervish of a dog with the obsessive-compulsive tendencies of a Border collie — *Are you going to throw that ball, are you? Okay, I will just wait here all day until you throw that ball. But when are you going to throw that ball?* — and the emotional profile of a Dalmatian. Which is to say, she was a diva: the world revolved around her and her alone. I could equally well have named her Diva, but ultimately Brydie was the perfect name: it was short for Bridget Mary, which gave her two names, befitting the somewhat contradictory personality she revealed herself to be. One name fit the times she was a calm and sweet Bridget, and the other fit the times she was a crazed, attacking Mary. But after she lit into that dog in the training session, I panicked and made a faulty assumption: I decided she was a bad dog whom I would need to keep away from other dogs. I didn't know that much about dogs at the time and had never had a really difficult dog, so perhaps I could be excused somewhat for making this error in judgment. Yet in so doing I led Brydie and myself down the rabbit hole.

It was really scary taking her for a walk after that. I lived in an area with a lot of dogs. We had one trail where everyone walked their dogs, and when I walked Brydie on it, I felt I had to call out and warn people (who didn't already know) that I had a crazed and vicious dog, and they should not let their dog come up and say hi. To her credit, Brydie would be fine on the leash walking around other dogs until that precise moment when some unsuspecting dog got just within her lunge-reach, at which point Brydie would explode outward. Walking your dog is supposed to be fun and relaxing; walking Brydie, unless there was no one else on the dog path, was hardly that.

This went on for about six months. I gave up on dog classes, feeling that I was on my own with no options. Then one day another dog walker, seeing how pathetic Brydie and I were, made a fateful comment: "You know, your dog is just feeding off of your thoughts and your reactions. You can change that behavior." That was the day the world shifted for Brydie and me. I took that statement to heart and set about finding the way to fix the problem that apparently I had somehow created.

I discovered that when I let someone else take Brydie's leash — someone who was confident and calm, with lots of dog experience — and walk her up to another dog, Brydie would be fine. She could be a little growly with raised back hair at first, but fairly quickly she started playing. Who knew? My Alien Dog was actually more of a life-of-the-party girl. To fix the situation, when I walked her and we approached another dog on-leash, I closed my eyes, turned the other way, breathed deeply, and focused on pleasant thoughts. Holding the leash, I'd say, "Brydie, be nice." Then after a few seconds, I would chance a peek to see if the other dog was still standing. Almost invariably, Brydie would be down in a doggie bow to her new friend or hopping around and cajoling the dog to play.

I finally came to see that when I was scared, Brydie got scared; she was reading my body language, my feelings, and my thoughts, and acting accordingly. When she was with someone calm and unperturbed, she was a different dog. Right about the time this was all occurring with Brydie, I made the decision to quit my part-time job as an environmental consultant and become a full-time animal communicator. I already understood and accepted that my dog could read my thoughts and feelings. What took me longer to comprehend was the fact that Brydie was actually reflecting or mirroring aspects of my own persona back to me by her unwelcome behavior. Eventually, in order to remedy Brydie's aggression, I had to face my part in creating it. She not only mirrored my fear and apprehension, but she showed me some subtle truths that ran as unnoticed undercurrents in the situation.

For instance, if I had not jumped to conclusions, refused to get help, and decided that all hope was lost, Brydie and I would not have spent six months in dog-walk hell. The situation with Brydie became a crisis because of how I chose to react, and upon closer examination, I realized this was how I unconsciously reacted to many of life's challenges. In time, of course, I identified how my experiences growing up led to that kind of knee-jerk reaction in me, and I had to forgive myself for not being perfect. What was really fascinating, though, was how the situation with Brydie exposed this syndrome to the open air so that I could work to heal and change my outmoded crisis-response thinking. In particular, Brydie's behavior revealed my own ambivalence toward and mistrust of other dog owners. In the past, I had had a few bad encounters with dogs attacking my dogs, and I unconsciously assumed that the threat of aggressive dogs and irresponsible dog owners was universal. In fact, in the neighborhood where I lived with Brydie, this was a relatively minor issue. Internally, I anticipated problems, conflict, and difficulty from other dogs and dog owners. What Brydie was actually doing by attacking other dogs was demonstrating for me all the negative feelings and thoughts that were churning away undiscovered, not inside her, but inside me!

My Animal My Self charts new territory in the world of human and animal relationships. It shows you in detail how mirroring between animals and people happens. By mirroring I don't mean behavioral mirroring that occurs when an animal copies a movement or sound made by a human, and I'm not referring to an animal reacting to the signals put out by a person's body language. Rather, I'm talking about the kind of mirroring Brydie did with me. She was not only reading my body language; she could feel my fear and apprehension and actually see my mental pictures as I imagined her attacking another dog.

The field of animal communication is based on the assumption that it is possible for you and your animal to communicate intuitively by picking up each other's thoughts, feelings, experiences, and mental images. Animals are the masters of this skill. I am an animal communicator by profession, which means I communicate this way with animals every day. I have written three books about this subject, and each book helps you understand how animal communication works and gives you instructions and exercises for doing it yourself. In each book I also go into detail about how you can know when communication is real and valid, and I give lots of examples, in the form of stories, of how people have discovered for themselves that it is authentic. I have proven to myself without a doubt that animal communication is possible, and I have taught thousands of people this skill, so I know it is something that everyone can master with good instruction and a little practice.

In *My Animal, My Self* I assume the reader accepts the validity of animal communication. If this concept is completely new to you, I encourage you to read one of my other books to learn more about it and discover how to do this yourself with your own animals. However, the idea that we can communicate intuitively with animals has been prevalent and popular in modern culture for about twenty years now, so it shouldn't really surprise anyone anymore. One researcher, the British microbiologist Rupert Sheldrake, has proved through statistically verified experiments that animals can read our minds from a distance. He has shown that a dog can predict, through his behavior, when his person makes the decision to head toward home, without any possibility of an environmental clue tipping the dog off. Sometimes people criticize research into animal communication as anecdotal, but Sheldrake has pointed out that many accepted scientific conclusions are based on anecdotes. Studies of drugs used to reduce pain rely on patient anecdotes, in which there is no measure of proof beyond what patients report. Accumulate enough anecdotes, and this becomes quantifiable scientific data. At this point, the wealth of books and articles about the accuracy and verifiability of animal communication should have addressed any questions about whether it exists. I am not saying that every animal communicator is accurate, nor even that the good ones are accurate all the time. I am simply saying that animals and people, even though they can't speak the same verbal language, can communicate and understand one another through intuitive communication.

What's new about what I offer in this book — and what I find intriguing — is the concept that our animals consciously, and even at times purposely, reflect back to us what is going on inside us, including our beliefs, our emotions, and even our physical condition. They can read our minds and hearts directly, without external clues, and even when we ourselves are unconscious of our thoughts and feelings, our animals will, at times, deliberately act these out for our benefit — to show us what we can't see ourselves. This is what I believe was happening between Brydie and me.

Through mirroring, Brydie showed me how completely incorrect and inadequate my thinking was about her. She reflected for me the error of my approach to her in particular, and to life in general. This is just one aspect of the mirroring that can occur between people and animals — the process whereby animals show us what's not working in our lives, what's dysfunctional, what's not fun. At this point, it's important to ask, why would an animal do something like that? Why didn't Brydie just ignore what I was feeling and thinking and go have a blast with other dogs? This is a key question to understanding how mirroring can occur. Using the case of Brydie to illustrate, initially there was an external aspect of her personality that needed some adjusting to get her to a level of ease and compatibility with other dogs.

As I mentioned, she had the personality of a diva, an *I'm-too-good-for-you-to-approach-me* attitude toward other dogs. This was something I needed to work through with her, and if I had had a clue, it would have been fairly easy to do with a little training. In later years, all I would do when Brydie acted huffy was say, "Brydie, chill out and act nice." She would then instantly turn into the perfect angel.

But on a deeper level, it was the emotional bond between us that compelled her to act in ways that would, eventually, make both of us happier. She became my teacher, helping me see that the way I was viewing life was really not much fun and wasn't producing good results. Brydie also acted as my healer, helping me fix a situation that was not doing either of us any good. In a direct practical way, she also brought me tools for my profession, since the things I used to change her hyperness and reactivity — clicker training, Tellington TTouch bodywork, and other natural, nonviolent training techniques[1] — were things I needed to know to be able to help my clients and *their* animals.

This book is an examination of the many ways that our animals reflect back to us what is going on inside us emotionally, mentally, physically, and spiritually, and the reasons animals do this. This bond between ourselves and our animals is the foundation of mirroring. The bond comes about because of the enormous capacity for empathy that animals have, far exceeding that of most humans. Once they enter our lives, our animals become inextricably linked to our emotional network. The bond Brydie and I established in our first months together meant that she could not help but be in sync with my emotions. That's just what animals do. This capacity to bond is what makes animals so helpful in therapy situations, such as when psychologists use animals in sessions with traumatized children. This bonding behavior is also what can compel your animal to mirror your thoughts, emotions, and physical issues back to you, in an attempt to help you heal. Unless an animal has been severely abused, she will not shut down her heart to a human. In the world of humans, the opposite is true. We are conditioned by modern culture to shut off our feelings, including those of empathy and compassion. Animals can't do that. If they are unhappy, they don't go looking for ways to suppress that feeling, as humans would. They look for ways to become happy again, and because of the bond they have with us, they won't be happy unless we are happy. Our animals will do all they can to show us how we are not happy — what beliefs, habits, actions, and emotions we have that are not working. Your animal can love you so much he or she will actually mimic your physical issues and even try to heal you by taking on your injury or disease. By really understanding this process, as this book will help you to do, you will discover that your relationship with your animal is much deeper and more pervasive in every aspect of your life than you ever imagined.

The process of mirroring is not just about illuminating problems or dysfunctions; animals show us our positive aspects as well.

It's important to see that balance and to recognize all the positive correlations between you and your animal. But when something isn't broken, we typically don't notice it. We only really pay attention when something isn't working well, so understandably many of the stories in this book will be about mirroring of negative emotions and thoughts that need a bit of adjustment.

It's all well and good when you can see and correct a negative mirroring dynamic as easily as I did with Brydie, but what if it is not so obvious? How exactly does one get at this issue and fix it? That's where this book offers a breakthrough for animal lovers, by giving a complete guide to how to discover and analyze mirroring between you and your animal and showing methods to address negative mirroring using a variety of techniques. With Brydie, I knew our problems were a thing of the past when one day I came upon a crowd of dog owners and their dogs hanging out in one of the fields adjacent to the dog path. The dogs were all off-leash and romping around having a great time; the owners were looking on fatuously, as dog owners will. I unclipped Brydie's leash, watched her rush headfirst into the fray, and called after her, "Go play, Brydie, but be chill!" She started her rounds by going up to one of the dogs and doing what I call "the porpoise," which involved butting her nose into the dog's chest to get the dog, whom she may actually have perceived more as a wind-up toy, to go. I did mention the diva thing, right? At this juncture I called out, "Easy, Brydie!" and she immediately backed off. Instead, she switched to crazed running and began tracking a huge circle around the group of dogs until she had them all following her at breakneck pace, at which point she led them in a grand parade through the field, looking back occasionally to make sure all her ducks were lined up: my party girl!

My friend Gerrie Huijts, whose persistent interest helped make this book happen, is fond of saying, "Everything is about mirroring." What she means is that everything that happens to you in your life — including the activities you choose to engage in, the people and animals around you, and your experiences, both good and bad — are a mirror for your feelings and thoughts. This can be a very daunting concept until you experience how completely liberating it is. Since how we humans live our lives can so deeply impinge upon our animals' lives, I would be remiss if I did not cover that topic in this book as well. So in the Conclusion you will learn how to address and remedy the situation if the mirror of your life is not exactly as you wish it to be.

Through the Animal Looking Glass

In 2008, a group of dog trainers in Hungary got together for six hours with their dogs and made a YouTube video that has now garnered almost eight million hits. Called "A Doggy Christmas Surprise,"[1] the video shows a group of dogs who, left alone in a Budapest apartment, decide to roll up the rugs and decorate the tree while their humans are gone. Set to the tune of "Rockin' Around the Christmas Tree," the dogs climb ladders, hang ornaments, dress each other up in Christmas decorations, put garlands on the tree from the top down, and line the bottom of the tree with presents. It's clear throughout that they are having a rocking good time: no bad-dog-do-it-again feeling to this video. The dogs are featured in another equally popular video called "A Doggy Summer," where they show up at the beach minus their humans and have a beach party, setting up umbrellas, tossing Frisbees, and lounging around on the sand and in the water. The trainers had no idea that these videos would become YouTube sensations, but because the dogs are now world famous, so is the technique that was used to train them, called the "Mirror Method." It's based on the tendency for dogs to mirror or imitate and follow the behavior of their trainers.[2]

This group of Hungarian dog trainers belong to the Dogschool of Népsziget. They have gone on to do many YouTube videos of their public training events, and they are emphatic in their belief that everything you observe about a dog is really a reflection of the owner: whatever is going on for a dog, good or bad, is about what is going on for the owner, and to fix it, one must look to the owner, not the dog.

What they describe as the Mirror Method has three parts. The first part is for the human to create a bond and respect between him or herself and the dog and then to start mirroring the desired behavior. The second aspect is to use positive reinforcement clicker training, working with the dog off-leash to shape the desired behavior. The third component is lifestyle, where the dog is encouraged to be a real dog and allowed to romp in the woods, bite, wrestle, and generally have a good time in dog terms. The formation of this school and this highly effective method of training was a direct result of mirroring between the founder, Gabor Korom, and his competition dog. Gabor was a world-champion Schutzhund[3] competitor, but he was so obsessed with winning that his dog became sick. He quit the sport and turned instead to examining the human–canine relationship; in the process he discovered the dynamic of mirroring. As a result of his dog becoming ill due to such intense competition, Gabor found the way to train dogs so that they love every minute of it.

The idea that we have to look to the person if there are problems with the animal is echoed by nonviolent, natural horse trainers like Buck Brannaman, who was made famous by the 2011 documentary *Buck*. Brannaman agrees with Gabor that when a human and an animal form a relationship, the animal will behave in ways that are directly related to some of the traits of the human. These can include both positive traits like calmness and playfulness and negative traits like fear and aggression. He says people come to his clinics thinking they are going to fix their horses and then find out that they really need to fix themselves. One of Brannaman's now-famous quotes sums it up: "The horse is a mirror to your soul. Sometimes you might not like what you see. Sometimes you will." To Brannaman, any "issue" with a horse is usually not about the horse at all; rather, it's about what the horse is *reflecting back about the owner.*[4]

I haven't found any cat-training groups, like the dog trainers in Hungary, that claim badly behaved cats to be the fault of their correspondingly badly behaved humans, but the same principles apply whether we are talking about dogs, cats, or iguanas: animals who bond with a human counterpart will be influenced in a profound way by that association. Never is this more evident to me than in the occasional call I get from someone with a persistently out-of-control cat who is biting, attacking, or otherwise slashing at them tooth and claw. And for certain, when I find that the cat has been this way for years, and I learn that the person attached to the cat is hesitant to upset or interfere with the cat regardless of the behavior, I know I am dealing with an out-of-balance mirroring situation. Each animal is different, of course. Horses will nip at you or walk right at you to move you out of the way — that is just their nature. Dogs are much easier, as they truly just want to please their humans and will do almost anything to accomplish that. But cats seem to assume a who-gives-a-damn-about-you attitude; they will most definitely tend to claw and bite if they are not pleased, and humans need to find the best ways to counteract this "cat abuse," for lack of a better term. Becoming aware of the dynamic of mirroring is an essential element.

My first introduction to the concept of mirroring was through Dr. Marty Goldstein's book *The Nature of Animal Healing: The Path to Your Pet's Health, Happiness, and Longevity.* He explains from the point of view of a holistic veterinarian why animals get sick and how we can prevent that. I have been following his guidance for over fifteen years with great success, and I recommend Dr. Goldstein's book to my clients. Although he wrote the book about cats and dogs, the principles he espouses — avoid chemicals, drugs, and vaccines when possible, consume whole organic foods — can be applied to all animals, including humans. Goldstein emphasizes that illness can have its origin in one's beliefs and emotions; in other words, most disease starts as a mental/emotional condition before it manifests in the body. I came to personally understand this through my own experience with a severe back injury, but until I started working as an animal communicator, I didn't completely understand the pervasiveness of the interplay between disease and our internal reality. The way Dr. Goldstein explains it makes a lot of sense: most organisms have at least one genetic weakness present. Stress, emotional turmoil, and negative beliefs can affect the weak genetic links in a body, whether that weakness be in one's heart, bladder, or joints, or in a genetic predisposition for cancer. Tension and stress trigger the inherent weaknesses unique to each individual. However, if you stay happy, calm, and have abundant energy and a great attitude, it is much less likely that these weaknesses will be triggered.

When you start to search for and analyze the phenomenon of mirroring, you see it everywhere: it makes sense that it would occur, for instance, in couples, who come to resemble each other over time, engage in the same hobbies, have the same opinions, and even adopt each other's speech patterns. One can also observe mirroring between parents and children.

An Overlooked Phenomenon

Mirroring is not a new concept, but it appears to be an overlooked idea. In psychology, the concept of projection is similar to mirroring, but it does not capture the reciprocity of mirroring. When people project their own beliefs, fears, expectations, and so on onto others, it's considered a one-way process, in which the other party isn't really directly involved. The process of mirroring, in contrast, is reciprocal, and involves causality, as each party is affected by the other in an ongoing and potentially shifting dynamic.

Psychodrama, a therapeutic technique in which the therapist and client re-create a past traumatic situation in order to heal long-standing damage, is, in a way, analogous to what happens when an animal mirrors a human. Mirroring re-creates the seen and un-seen dynamics of our inner lives, and when negative aspects of this are brought to our awareness, it can be immediately healing. If you look for it, you can see people unconsciously creating their own psychodramas and mirroring situations all the time in their every-day lives: in their choice of partners, friends, jobs, places to live, and even in their choice of companion animals. Of course, we don't realize we are doing this unless we stop and really take a look at our lives — something most people don't do.

When I went searching for books, articles, and analyses on mir-roring, I found a lot of information on the metaphysical aspects, including the idea that everything in life is a mirror, but nothing in the field of psychology. One good book I found is *Living in the Light,* by Shakti Gawain,[5] which is an in-depth guide on how to work with the concept that the world is your mirror, as a way to improve your life. There is virtually nothing written about mirroring between animals and people. Even within the field of animal communica-tion, mirroring is not that well known or understood.

Defining Mirroring Between People and Animals

In all our relationships, a subconscious interplay exists between ourselves and the other, be it human or animal, and an overlap of our energy fields. Dr. Goldstein calls this interplay *resonance*; I call it *mirroring.*

Mirroring can result in both parties acting in ways that reflect what is going on inside one or the other, and it can sometimes be very simple and direct. A person who is calm and deals with his or her animal calmly will probably have a calm animal — if not right away, then eventually, as the animal comes into sync with the person. Mirroring can also be more subtle than this. A striking example was told to me by my friend and colleague Carol Gurney[6] about a man who was an alcoholic. Every time the man would go on a binge, his dog would have a seizure, and he would have to interrupt the binge to take the dog to the veterinary clinic. Finally, after several such events, it dawned on him that his dog was getting seizures only and at the precise moment when he would start a drinking binge. That was enough to make him stop, and when he stopped drinking, the dog stopped having seizures. No one in the man's family had been able to get him to stop drinking, an intervention hadn't worked, but that dog did it. Animals can go places in our hearts that no one else can reach. The outcome in this case was a return to what all animals fundamentally want: love, comfort, harmony with their people, and happiness. These are the things, it seems to me, that are always the objects of an animal's mirroring.

Not every behavior by one's animal is an instance of mirroring. For example, I recently rescued an older white quarter horse mare who had been severely abused by someone who was clearly a rageaholic. It took me almost two months to be able to get close to her without having to trap her first. This horse's fear is a reaction to her past ill treatment; it is not a direct mirror for me. I'm not sure yet what mirroring is occurring between that mare and me. The answer may lie in the reasons why I saved and adopted her: I felt sorry for her, as she was not having any fun and she was the true love of the mustang I adopted as my trail horse — and I didn't want to see them separated. Over time I will learn more about how she and I mirror each other. In fact, as a way to explore this, I chose her as the focus of the mirroring questionnaire sample report I present in chapter 6 (see page 133). For now, it's enough to know that she is becoming happy and content and that she trusts me to the extent that I can do the things I need to take care of her.

In addition, not every animal's illness is a reflection of mirroring, as was the case in the dog story above. As a biologist I am keenly aware of how polluted the earth is. Any animal can become ill because of an environmental hazard, like drinking water polluted by fracking,[7] or from eating contaminated commercial food. In the bigger picture, however, the condition of the earth may actually be a mirror for humanity, and we should consider the significance of the fact that we are destroying the environment, supporting toxic food industries, and so on.

Aspects of Mirroring

Positive, Negative, Neutral

When we look in the mirror, we tend to feel one of three basic things: positive, negative, or neutral. Sometimes we like what we see, sometimes we don't. Sometimes what we once liked we don't anymore. Mirroring the way I am discussing it is no different. Mirroring is a dynamic. It can show you the good qualities that you and your animal share. For example, people who love Jack Russell terriers or Arabian horses tend to have lots of energy, just like those breeds. Having lots of energy is often a good thing, unless it escalates into being hyperenergetic. Too much energy becomes a negative situation when it leads to being stressed out and getting stress-related illness. Mirroring can also be neutral, for instance, when an owner with red hair chooses only red-haired animals. This sort of mirroring does no harm. However, when the mirroring dynamic between ourselves and our animals exhibits some negative aspect about what we are doing or how we are feeling, that's when we may want to shift things to be more positive.

For example, without realizing it, I was being too overprotective of my dog Toby, who is a chiweiner (a Chihuahua and dachshund cross). I discovered this from a student during a teleclass I was teaching. The students in the class were talking intuitively from a distance with Toby. I asked them to see if Toby had a message for me. One student relayed the message from Toby that he wanted to be treated more like a dog and be more free like Norman, my other dog who is a beagle. I immediately realized the truth of this statement. Often mirroring between ourselves and our animals, especially negative mirroring, is hard to see; it is the nature of the dynamic. It is hard for us to see our own weaknesses and nonproductive behaviors. We would prefer to see ourselves as perfect, or nearly so.

For a variety of reasons, I was not letting Toby run free on my ranch, as I was with Norman. For one thing, Toby is smaller and can fit through the holes in the sheep fencing. Toby also has a tendency to run away, so I was worried he would slip through the fence and

Toby

take off. Also, I never had a little dog before; they require a lot more care and fussing than other dogs, and one can easily become over-protective with them. Looking deeper, I realized that I see Toby more like a human baby than a dog. I never had a baby, and he is the first animal I have had who really feels like a baby to me, even though he is four years old. I am sure I was being more protective of him because Toby is the closest I will ever come to that experience. I decided that I didn't want to be overprotective of Toby. I wanted him to have fun in life. I told my student she was spot on, 100 percent accurate in her communication. Afterward, I took Toby outside with Norman and told him that from now on he would get the same freedoms Norman got. I let them both off-leash, and they raced down to the barn. Now I let him off-leash twice a day to run with Norman, and as a result Toby is much healthier and happier and he always comes right back when I call him.

When describing mirroring, instead of *positive* and *negative*, I could use the words *balanced* and *unbalanced*, but it all comes to the same thing. Some things your animal shows you will be great and some will be not so great. The important point is to work on shifting the things you are not happy with, then they will change for the better. In this way, negative mirroring can become positive, and all negative mirroring can be seen as part of the process for creating positive mirroring.

Mirroring can result from conscious choice. For example, I love Arabian horses because they are so smart, and I find it hard to resist super-smart animals. The mirror in this case could either be that I am attracted to what is a match inside me, or that I am attracted to something I lack but would love to have. Mirroring can also result from some unconscious process. As an example, without knowing this beforehand, I seem to always choose horses who have meta-bolic syndrome (that is, they can't eat a high-carbohydrate diet), just like me.

What exactly is being mirrored, and what if anything to do

about it, always depends on the person and the animal involved. People often choose certain breeds because of the breed characteristics and the look of the animal. As with the example of me choosing smart animals, this could be an attraction to animals who have qualities that we like in ourselves, or it could be an attraction to something we would like to possess. Perhaps the quality that draws us is clearly positive, such as an animal who is friendly to everyone, or perhaps it is seemingly negative, like an animal who is aggressive or standoffish. Such an animal may be a match for the person's own internal fear. When a person chooses an animal with similar issues and characteristics, it could be an effort to feel accepted and avoid being judged. For instance, if an antisocial person adopts a dog who is equally antisocial, the person might find comfort in this. Or the person may choose this type of animal in an unconscious effort to resolve this specific life challenge. The world is full of such stories.

Lisa and Bella

My holistic veterinarian, Dr. Lisa Pesch, told me this story about the challenge presented by her cat, Bella, who had always been a bit standoffish to people. At one point, Bella started attacking people, particularly two people who were regular visitors to Lisa's home. Lisa's partner at the time commented, "Wow, Bella acts just like you." At first, Lisa said she could not see that at all and was in total denial. Then, in time, she saw the accuracy of the observation and recognized the mirroring going on. The two people Bella particularly didn't like were people Lisa also didn't particularly like, but she would not let herself be honest about this. So instead, Bella acted out those feelings by attacking these two people. Once Lisa saw the correlation, she assured Bella that the message was received, and she found a way to be more straightforward with the visitors. Soon after, the attacks by Bella stopped.

Lisa and Bella

Direct and Indirect Mirroring

As these examples make clear, direct mirroring is much easier to see. We are angry at someone, and our animal acts aggressively toward them; we have a bad back and our animal has a bad back. Even so, it can be hard to make these connections ourselves, which are sometimes so obvious others can't imagine why we aren't seeing it. Dr. Goldstein tells the story of an overweight couple coming into his office so he could treat their equally overweight basset hound. Somehow the connection was not being made.

Indirect mirroring is even harder to recognize and identify. It can require some patience and digging in order to understand what your animal's condition or behavior is mirroring. I spent years working to heal my Arabian horse, Dylan, of metabolic syndrome and bad feet to no avail. But because of all that was wrong with his body, and all the things I investigated to try to heal him, I learned a huge amount about holistic care for horses. I studied barefoot trimming and horse bodywork to an extent that I can now do both modalities myself. I am convinced that my mirroring dynamic with Dylan was partly to lead me in the direction of holistic care and natural horsemanship so that I could help other horse owners with their horses.

With an indirect mirroring situation, it's as if the mirror is clouded. A person who is fearful of other people, and whose dog becomes aggressive to strangers, may have no clue that the dog's aggression is really an expression of the fear that person feels internally. But it is very common for your animal to act out and behave inappropriately as a way to mirror something that is out of balance in you or your life.

The Four Modes of Mirroring

The complex aspects of mirroring occur within four distinct categories or modes — physical, mental, emotional, and spiritual. I define these modes individually below, but in reality they can blend into each other. A physical mirror situation, like a sick animal who is reflecting a stressed-out owner, can lead to a spiritual awakening: the person might realize that to resolve the tension for herself and her animal, she has to change occupations or get rid of an abusive partner. This kind of blending and flowing from one mode into another is common. Understanding each of the different modes of mirroring can help you determine what types of mirroring may be occurring between you and your animal.

Physical

The most basic physical mirroring is the direct matching of appearance, temperament, and behavior — for example, the person who has golden wavy hair that looks exactly like the coat of her golden retriever. There can also be a direct connection between our physical health and that of our animals.

Tina Hutton, a bodyworker for humans and horses who is certified in CMT, TTouch, and Feldenkrais methods,[8] is in the business of spotting and addressing negative, direct physical mirroring. She told me of one instance when she was asked by a riding instructor to evaluate a client's progress during a riding lesson. The instructor had observed that the rider was collapsed on one side of the torso, with the leg on that side rising upward in a clenched manner. Tina could see that this position affected how the horse traveled, creating a slightly curved pattern in the horse's movement. At Tina's suggestion, they wrapped an ace bandage around the rider's leg, from the foot up to the hip area, to invite more internal awareness of the leg's clenched condition to the rider. The rider was hesitant about using the wrap, but immediately upon riding with it in place, that side of her body began to change. Her instructor was amazed at the difference. Even before the rider sensed the change, her horse knew: the mare became straighter and more balanced as she walked across the arena.

Mirroring on the physical level can lead to an animal taking on an illness or disease of the owner. Every holistic animal practitioner I interviewed for this book agreed that this happens in their practice regularly. If you discover, doing the exercises in this book, that your animal may be taking on your physical issues, you certainly want to correct that, and I give methods for addressing and reversing such a situation.

Mental

In the case of my dog Brydie, the more I mentally constructed my image of her as a crazed monster, the more she fitted herself to that role. Because animals have no barriers to our thoughts, they can't help but absorb them. This is true for many humans, too. People who are highly sensitive will pick up on thoughts from others and can be influenced unduly by them. But humans can choose to leave or distance themselves physically; animals cannot. Of course, it is sometimes hard to decide what influence a thought has versus an emotion, as thoughts and emotions are usually coupled. While I discuss them separately here, in real life distinguishing them isn't critical. When analyzing what is going on with you and your animal, you just need to identify what is happening, not what box to fit it in.

When I asked my friend Morgan, who likes to go trail riding with me whenever we get a chance, if she had a story she might like to share in this book, she told me about two negative thoughts that plague her when riding and that relate to difficulties with her horse. I didn't even realize she had these issues, as she is a very good rider and a competent horse person. To my surprise, she told me that she is both claustrophobic and afraid of taking horses through water. When faced with loading a horse in a trailer, she immediately has the mental image of the walls of the trailer closing in on her. One of the techniques for intuitive animal training is to imagine, in a mental movie, what you want an animal to do. Well, imagining *that* scenario would not be the best way to get a horse to jump into a trailer. Now I understood why every time we trailered to ride, we had to go through a few tricks to get her horses in the trailer. It was the same thing with water: you can lead a horse to a creek, but you can't get them to cross if you are imagining a sea monster hidden in the depths waiting to bite their feet off.

What we think and believe can have a huge impact on our animals at a very deep level, affecting their emotional state, their behavior, and even their health. It doesn't help that we are sometimes unconscious of our beliefs and aren't even aware of what they are. The techniques in this book will help you first identify negative beliefs that may be adversely affecting your animal, and then shift those beliefs to be more positive in order to restore balance for you and your animal.

Emotional

Animals will respond to your emotional state, even if you think you are hiding your feelings and not displaying them outwardly. Animals are masters at connecting intuitively — they know everything we think and feel. We have no secrets from our animals, as the following story illustrates.

KOEKIE AND TESSA

Tessa Montanus is in her twenties and lives alone with three dogs. She sought help from my colleague Gerrie Huijts because her dog Koekie was becoming aggressive and attacking other dogs and even people. Tessa was forthcoming about the fact that she lived alone in order to avoid other people. Tessa said that Koekie would become too easily stimulated around others and would overreact. Then Tessa had the realization that, if she were a dog, she would behave in a similar fashion to Koekie. Like her dog, Tessa didn't trust people and she was angry all the time. Tessa could see that this mirroring was a detriment to both of them, and it spurred Tessa to change her feelings and her lifestyle. She didn't want to condemn her dog or herself to staying holed up in a house, unable to go out, isolated from others. Tessa told me she sought out therapy and coaching to help her ease her mistrust of people and of life. She worked to change her attitudes and beliefs so that Koekie would not feel unsafe when out in public. Slowly, with support, time, and patience, she and Koekie have

Koekie

begun venturing out more and having more fun. Tessa's life would not have improved, and Koekie may have been labeled a vicious dog, if Tessa had not been able to finally see the mirror image her dog was showing her.

DOUBLE THAT FOR HORSES

Horses are like the ultimate Rorschach test because, as prey animals, they are constantly on alert and ready to charge off if there is danger. How you feel around a horse will almost instantly be seen in the horse's behavior. Horse expert Tina Hutton had this to say:

> A person who is fearful may treat the horse like a toy poodle, hugging it and giving lots of treats. While some horses may indeed be the kind to manage all situations by being the "leader" for their humans, others may resort to any number of other behaviors. Some may become bullies to their humans, some may ignore the human and seek their own desires, and some may develop their own fearful reactions to life that match the owner.
>
> In order to survive the rapid changes or confusing information from humans, some horses may try to shut down their responses. Other horses are likely to build up tension levels that match or exceed what the owner projects. Both cases may lead to rides that are not what the owners had in mind. In severe cases, the results can become dangerous for both parties.[9]

To help horse owners undo a bad situation, Tina has them slow down, using "calming signals" derived from the work of dog behaviorist Turid Rugaas and the breathing techniques of Michael Grant White. Tina Hutton is also a practitioner of TTEAM (Tellington TTouch Equine Awareness Method),[10] a horse training method developed by Linda Tellington-Jones, which trains the horse owner to learn the body language of horses and shows people how to teach a horse to learn rather than just how to respond to a stimulus. Through helping people interpret horse body language, Tina helps them understand why their horses are reacting poorly, how the horse is feeling, and what the owner has to do to elicit a better response. When owners are willing to observe the dynamics of every step of handling, training, and riding their horses, they gain more understanding about horses and learn how to convey ideas with clarity and respect. The reward for following these practices is the joy of being in harmony in the moment with the horse.

Spiritual

Many people talk about how an animal saved their lives, got them out of depression, or made them move toward a better future. Few animal lovers will deny that animals change their lives for the better. When an animal is mirroring on a spiritual level, usually something profound and life changing comes out of it — an outcome that transports the person to a new level of existence in their lives. This story of Yuri and Rudy is one such spiritual journey.

YURI AND RUDY

Yuri Shimojo came into my life when she signed up for one of my animal communication teleclasses shortly after the 2011 tsunami in Japan. We quickly discovered a shared concern with the continuing crisis surrounding the meltdowns of Japan's nuclear power plants. Yuri is an artist and activist and one of those people I identify as a free spirit, whom it is always so nice to encounter.[11] Months later, I got the chance to meet Yuri and Rudy in person when I went to New York to teach a workshop. In the class, Yuri and her dog were both happy and friendly. Yuri greeted and connected with the other students and became the class favorite; Rudy got all the dogs playing, chasing each other, and generally having great fun. They were both extroverted and confident — you would never have guessed that they started out their journey together from quite a different place.

If left to her own devices, Yuri would not have gotten Rudy. She and her partner were not planning to have children, so Yuri was surprised when one day her partner announced he wanted to get a dog as "their baby." She was also hesitant about the decision, as they were both artists who traveled frequently; a dog would mean commitment and could hamper the freedom of their lifestyle, but she decided to go along with the plan because she had been wanting a dog again in her life.

Yuri had had a Pekinese as a child and wanted another one, but her partner wanted a boxer. They compromised on a Boston terrier, one from a pet store, since her partner didn't want a rescue dog, though Yuri did.

The Pekinese Yuri had as a child helped her survive the loss of her father, and months before getting Rudy, a psychic channeler said the dog would return to her one day. But Yuri was not expecting to reconnect with her childhood companion, especially since they were not getting the same breed.

Yuri and Rudy (photo by Maki Kaoru)

They found Rudy, a three-month-old Boston terrier, in what Yuri described as a Brooklyn ghetto pet store. In retrospect Yuri realized that Rudy was born in some puppy mill around the time when the channeler had said her old dog would return to her in this life. When they got Rudy home, they realized that he was not a happy, uncomplicated baby substitute. Instead he was terrified of everything outside of his cage, which is where he had probably spent his entire young life.

Then, shortly after getting Rudy, the couple broke up. Yuri was on her own in the midst of a depression and an identity crisis and having to deal with a dog who was afraid of his shadow. Both of them were totally confused, and neither knew what to do. They were, she realized later, complete mirrors for each other. Yuri began dreading and fearing the outside world, and going outside of the apartment was increasingly difficult. For Rudy every part of the world was terrifying. He had never learned to walk on a floor; he reacted to a falling leaf like it was a monster out to get him.

But he had to go out to pee and poop, and someone had to take him. With no other recourse, Rudy and Yuri ventured daily into the abyss. Incrementally, Yuri coaxed her dog outside, helped him to tolerate the stimuli around him, whether on the subway, walking in the neighborhood, or sitting at the cafés. Having to take Rudy out saved Yuri from becoming a recluse, or worse, someone incapable of leaving her home. Together they encouraged each other, helped each other gain confidence, and made each other strong. As she says, "We found our guts together." He inspired her to walk out and stand tall.

Now, according to Yuri, Rudy is the funniest, most friendly "mayor" in her neighborhood. He loves to wrestle with big dogs, beats greyhounds in races, beats golden retrievers in swimming contests, and generally impresses people with his strength, pluckiness, and exuberance. He has no clue that he is a small dog. And Yuri is busy with her artwork and activism, traveling with Rudy, meeting people, and making plans. Yuri says no one believes her when she describes how she and Rudy used to be. Yuri now believes that Rudy is the spirit of her dog from childhood, returned to teach her and help her heal. She and Rudy are still mirrors for each other, but now what they see in the mirror is happiness.

Why Animals Are Such Good Mirrors

People who love animals know that there is something unique about the connection we can have with them. Love for an animal is often deeper and more intense than anything you may have felt for a person. That's why it is so hard on us when our animal dies. There is a void that nothing can fill.

Psychologist Margot Lasher has written two books on the subject of animals, empathy, and the unusual connection between animals and humans.[12] Lasher says that psychologists and psychiatrists have neglected the role of animals in our lives. The relationship between a person and an animal is not given significance. Yet for many people, their closest friend may be their animal.

What lies behind this intense connection between people and animals is the fact that animals love us in a way that most humans can't even aspire to. They love us no matter what we look like — that just isn't an issue for them. They don't care if we are rich and famous, another nonissue. They love us even if we are depressed or grouchy. Animals don't judge us by the standards of modern human society — they look into our hearts and see whether there is a pure light there that they can connect to. Once an animal catches on to your heart, he or she won't let go or shut down unless severely betrayed. Animals stay loyal to us and openhearted almost no matter what happens. This is an amazing fact. You will, if you are open to it, find true and abiding love in almost every companion animal you allow into your life. Obviously, many animals have been abused and are no longer so easy to get close to, but once you win their trust, these animals, too, can find the way to heal, open their hearts, and love you unconditionally. It's extraordinary, really, and nothing like the emotional obstacle course of human relationships. Lasher says animals' capacity for empathy is the reason for this unconditional love, and because of this empathy, in her words, "Animals never hurt us the way humans do." Animals might attack to defend themselves, but they don't purposely try to hurt our hearts, reject us, or make us feel inadequate the way people do. A severely abused animal will shut down, but no animal will ever try to make us feel unloved. Quite the opposite: animals want love to prevail on all fronts.

According to Lasher, animals are incapable of shutting down their hearts. They have to remain connected to everything in the environment in order to stay safe. Not knowing how another feels, for an animal, could result in death. The imperative for all nonhuman species is to stay completely connected to all that is happening in the world.

I believe this is actually the normal condition for human beings as well; human cultures untouched by the modern age have these same characteristics. Modern culture has mediated the human propensity to stay open emotionally. We have modern culture to thank for the fact that we can disassociate. As children we start out just like animals, with a totally open and accepting heart, and then that gets changed by the surrounding culture. We don't forget how it felt to have an open heart, and when we encounter it in animals, we are drawn to it and embrace it.

Since animals can't shut us out, and they don't have the ability, let alone the inclination, to ignore us the way a human would, they come into sync with us. In so doing, they become our mirror. That is why animals are so useful in therapy work. I have spoken to, and read about, many psychologists who use animals in the therapeutic setting. Their clients tend to trust and open up more to an animal than to a person. Indeed, it would be interesting to know how many therapists and bodyworkers have their animals sit in on their sessions and to study what contributions those animals make.

The results are well known for horses used in therapeutic riding programs: they bring hope, joy, and a sense of accomplishment to both children and adults. According to equine-assisted learning practitioner Dr. Beverley Kane,[13] animals respond to our true intentions, not to our stated intentions, or even to what we think our intentions are. It's what I tell my clients all the time — you have no secrets from your animals.

The second factor that makes animals such good mirrors is their proximity to us. In most cases our companion animals, our dogs and cats in particular, can't escape us. They live with us 24/7, surrounded by our thoughts and feelings, and affected by our actions and lifestyles. Imagine changing places with your dog or cat and seeing through their eyes what daily life is like. With horses it is a bit different, as they may be stabled away from home, but the owner is still their major interface with the world of humans.

What animals do as a result of being around us and exposed so intensely to our ways is to take on and mirror back to us what is going on with us. They become a looking glass for us to see ourselves. Whatever we feel, they feel. What we are thinking, they pick up intuitively and will react to. There are no barriers between us and our animals. They are like litmus paper, or mistletoe, or sponges. They will reflect and mirror what is going on inside us, which means that if they are being annoying or exasperating, it could be because of something going on in us. That is the essence of mirroring. They model our behavior, issues, thoughts, and beliefs because they are connected at all times to us from the deepest possible level of their hearts.

A Healing Journey

Recognizing and understanding mirroring is a magical journey. The undercurrents that may be present in our relationships with our animals have been too long left unexplored. By uncovering them we have everything to gain for the health and well-being of ourselves and our animals. Once you discover some imbalanced situation that involves mirroring, the next step is to find the way to resolve it.

When people can clearly see how what they are doing, feeling, and thinking affects their animals and may be causing problems, they usually want to change the situation. They want to know all the things they can do to shift conditions so they and their animals can be as happy and healthy as possible. The reason for taking the time to discover what mirroring may be going on between you and your animal is that by doing so you can make things better for both of you. Ultimately the process becomes a complex journey in healing.

In the next four chapters I will explain how mirroring works, using examples from friends, clients, and my own experience. Once you have a good foundation of understanding, you can better recognize any mirroring that may be going on between you and your animals. Then, chapter 6 provides an extensive questionnaire to help you gain insight into this process with regard to your own animals. In that chapter, I also summarize the research on how thoughts and emotions can have an effect on the body, specifically with reference to common problems seen in animals, and I provide a system for detecting any potential mirroring that may be happening. In chapter 7, I offer a series of techniques that you can use to address any negative mirroring you may discover that you decide you want to change.

A Word about Guilt

As we begin, it's important to emphasize that the point of uncovering mirroring is not to make you feel worse. When it comes to our animals, we can assume guilt much too easily. If you find something you want to shift, don't beat yourself up. It is not as if you did something on purpose to harm your animal — mirroring just happens. The fact that our animals can take on our issues on whatever level and to whatever extent is out of our control. This is the way it is. I will do my best to explain it, and if you are observant and use the techniques in this book, you should be able to remedy negative mirroring, or even avoid having your animals take on any of your negative qualities. But we cannot change their tendency to mirror; it is just who animals are. Finally, remember that feeling guilty serves little purpose — instead, work at adjusting negative mirroring and creating positive mirroring; that is the way to make you and your animal happier.

Exercise — Who Chose Whom?

To understand mirroring, you need to explore the idea that the things that happen in our lives with our animals are not random. The premise behind the concept of mirroring is that more often than not our animals come into our lives for a purpose. I also believe that the animals are pretty well aware of this from the outset, but humans are culturally conditioned not to see this aspect of life.

One way to begin to comprehend the nonrandomness of our encounters with animals is to look at how they made their way to us. Usually, in retrospect, most of these meetings feel more like fate than just a chance event. The initial reasons why we choose to adopt an animal are many and varied. We might like the way they look or act, or feel sorry for them because of their plight, or feel compelled to help them because of how they look at us. Think back to each animal who has been in your life. How did that animal come into your life, and what element of mirroring might have been at play? Whatever the ostensible reason, it's possible that there was some kind of mirroring going on. Complete the exercise below and see what you discover about the animals you chose to have in your life.

Why Did I Choose You?

At the top of a sheet of paper, write your animal's name. Next, describe when and how you met: Write down everything you can remember about how you found your animal, where you met, and how you met. For example, if you got your animal from the local animal shelter, can you recall why you came back to that animal? What made you focus on that specific animal over all the others? Maybe the animal chose you, and there was no way for you to resist. Just record anything and everything you can recall.

What about this connection may have been mirroring? One way to determine that is to circle anything you have written down that seems to match you in some way. Those circled items represent mirroring between you and your animal.

Finally, ask yourself, did you feel like there was some fate at play? Did you feel like the animal was seeking you out, or that the universe was arranging things to make it inevitable for you and that animal to meet?

You can repeat this exercise for every animal you have had in your life.

Our Animals, Ourselves

"One does not meet oneself until one catches the reflection from an eye other than human."
— LOREN EISLEY

The Nature of Animals

In the world of our ancient ancestors, animals had a different status and significance — often they were seen as relatives and equals. In her book *When Oracles Speak*,[1] Dianne Skafte describes how ancient societies also revered animals as oracles. Whole books were written on how to interpret the sounds of crows, people consulted bee hives and ancient trees for advice, and they journeyed hundreds of miles to visit the oracle of Delphi. Indigenous cultures had a greater respect for animals and an appreciation of their importance. These ancient cultures also believed in the spirits of animals and sought to connect with animal spirits through shamanic practices.

Shamanism is an ancient tradition common in most indigenous cultures. The shaman connects with the spirit world — the world of the spirits of the ancestors, deities, and the spirits of animals and nature — to gain spiritual insight and healing power. This was most often done through a deep connection with an animal spirit. Although animistic religions have been supplanted by modern religions, there has been a revival of shamanism in popular culture and of shamanic study and journeying to connect with the spirit world. Modern culture, and particularly mainstream science, holds a much more limited view of animals, generally considering them to be inferior to humans.

When I studied for my master's degree in biology, I did a seminar on the idea that cooperation, not competition, is the more prevalent force influencing the evolution of species. In nature, cooperation leads to much better results than competition both between and among species. It's not the biggest, strongest males who survive best. It's the group of auntie woodpeckers who help the nestlings grow up and keep them safe; it's the wildebeests, gazelles, and impalas who work as a team to ward off predators; and it's the animals who cooperate in colonies and extended families for survival.

When I presented my ideas in the seminar, a couple of the graduate students went ballistic, becoming emotional far beyond a normal disagreement over evolutionary theories. How dare I suggest that nineteenth-century biologist Charles Darwin's theories were not true!? The faculty advisor was equally dismissive. It was amazing to watch how vehemently people will cling to an outmoded, counterproductive idea. What those graduate students and the faculty member were defending was the simplified and mistaken idea, taken from Darwin's complex work, that the animal world is like a gladiator arena, in which only the strongest, swiftest, and most cunning live to fight another day. In Darwin's age and to Darwin's dismay, this view of nature contributed to the rise of unbridled competition and the development of large, now out-of-control corporations. That was also the era of America's first billionaire, John D. Rockefeller, who believed that his efforts to ruthlessly build up his Standard Oil monopoly were sanctioned by the inherent competitiveness of the natural order.

Scientist Peter Kropotkin, Darwin's contemporary, first put forward the idea that cooperation rather than competition is the guiding force in nature. Darwin came to think more like

Kropotkin in later years, but it was Kropotkin who initially took a strong position in favor of the force of cooperation in nature. To Kropotkin, animals who developed the habit of mutual aid were more fit and stood a better chance of surviving and thriving than those who didn't.

Now, over a hundred years since Kropotkin made his observations, most ecologists believe cooperation is more prevalent than competition in species interactions and evolution; one example is Janis Dickinson, an evolutionary biologist at the University of California, Berkeley.[2] But scientists in other disciplines and most people around the world still subscribe to the notion that life is about the survival of the fittest. In other words, the damage has been done. This point is critical because it is one of the cornerstones of our beliefs about animals and nature, and it is one of the many ways in which we limit and diminish the natural world, with the apparent seal of approval of mainstream science. People now have a mental conception of animals and nature as ruthless and competitive, when nothing could be further from the truth.

Many outmoded ideas about the nature of life and consciousness still exist. In his 2012 book *Science Set Free*,[3] Rupert Sheldrake, part of a growing group of maverick scientists who are leading the way toward a new enlightenment in science, does the world an enormous favor by arguing persuasively and comprehensively for the rejection of several antiquated dogmas. In particular, he takes issue with the scientific beliefs that the world is a machine made up of inanimate matter that has no consciousness; that consciousness is nothing but the physical activity of the brain; that nature is mechanical and purposeless; that reality is only material or physical; and that free will, psychic phenomena, and the concept of spirit are just illusions.

I've identified the additional following dogmas pertaining specifically to animals that need to be revised as well. They are concepts that are simply untrue, but that continue to be propagated by mainstream science and to a large extent accepted by popular culture.

Animals and Altruism

There is a popular belief that while humans are capable of taking actions motivated purely by altruism — defined as an unselfish regard for or devotion to the welfare of others — animals possess no such motivation. Sociobiologist Edward O. Wilson[4] theorized that cooperation in the animal world is a result of the benefit conferred to an individual through helping relatives (because they share some of the same genes). Helping some individual unrelated to oneself was considered, from an evolutionary standpoint, a purely accidental side effect. He proposed this to be the case for people as well, but his theories were not widely accepted with respect to human behavior. Animals on the other hand continue to be viewed as lacking in altruism and thus "lesser" beings than humans.

However, based on my work of over twenty years with animals and their people, I see animals working expressly to help their people, selflessly giving of themselves to support their humans. Mirroring can be an intense labor of love by the animal on behalf of the person. The altruism displayed by the animals through mirroring is often what then leads so many pet owners on a healing path. The animal heroes of our world don't just save their owners, they save neighbors and total strangers. Consider the story of the dog Ginny, who even went around saving cats.[5] While there are a few scientists who see the true nature of animals as altruistic, the majority of scientists still formally define animals as incapable of altruism. In fact, I think animals are more altruistic than most humans.

Animals and Feelings

With regard to animals and their capacity for emotion, there continues to be a raging controversy in science about whether animals' capacity to feel is equivalent to humans. Many scientists admit that animals possess some level of emotions, but they won't accept that these feelings could match the complexity, nuance, and depth of humans. They justify these false distinctions between humans and animals in spite of excellent arguments for emotional equivalency, such as those put forth by Jeffrey Masson in *When Elephants Weep* and by animal behaviorist and professor emeritus at the University of Colorado, Boulder, Marc Bekoff in *The Emotional Lives of Animals*.[6] Once again mainstream science is unwilling to concede that animals resemble humans in this regard, while most animal lovers know that our animals truly love us and that they have as full an array of emotions as we do.

In a 2009 article in the *Denver Post*,[7] Marc Bekoff identified a short list of observable emotional and ethical behaviors in dogs. These can, I believe, be extrapolated to apply to many animal species, and they contradict the conception of animals as incapable of complex feelings. To quote the article:

- Dogs have a sense of fair play. They dislike cheaters. They experience joy in play. They delight in friends. The big guys handicap themselves in games with little guys.
- Dogs get jealous when a rival gets more or better treats or treatment. They are resentful, unnerved or saddened by unfair behavior.
- They are made anxious by suspense. They get afraid.
- They are embarrassed when they mess up or do something clumsy.
- They feel remorse or regret when they do something wrong. They seek justice. They remember the bad things done to them but sometimes choose to forgive.
- Dogs have affection and compassion for their animal and human friends and family. They defend loved ones. They grieve their losses.
- They have hope.

Animals and Intelligence

Intelligence in animals is a bit trickier to address, as animals simply don't use their intelligence to do the things humans do, but there are plenty of arguments in favor of animal intelligence.[8] The way I see this is that the expression of intelligence is influenced by each species' imperative. Bees may well have an intelligence equivalent to ours; they just have different goals and different physical attributes. So their intelligence comes out in the form of bee hives. How incredibly intelligent is a bee hive?

Certainly people who live with animals know they are outsmarted by them on a daily basis; it's just the scientists who can't seem to figure all this out.

Animals and Souls

The denigrating notion that animals have no souls, or have lesser souls, is put forth by most of the major world religions. This too is a belief that permeates most of the cultures in the world, creating a separation between humans and animals and solidifying the conception of animals as lesser beings (not to mention nature, which is on the bottom of the rubbish heap).

I agree with Marc Bekoff's proposal: "If we have souls, our animals have souls. If we have free choice, they have it. If we can't know this for sure, let's give them the benefit of the doubt."[9]

Animals as Healers and Teachers

From my perspective, through the lens of the thousands of animals I have communicated with in the past twenty-five years, animals are actually more advanced than humans in some regards, not only in their capacity for empathy, but also in their ability to stay in tune with everything around them and their connection to the world of spirit.

The basis for these traits and the reason why we miss companion animals so much when they die is because they maintain an open heart at all times. They do this in part as a survival mechanism. To stay connected means you must keep your heart open and receiving; you can't shut your heart down. Animals do this so that they can, at any moment, know as much as possible about their environment, including the feelings of others. This is why we feel safe with the animals who share our lives and feel we can trust them implicitly. We know at a deep level that animals can't harm us the way people can. As Margot Lasher says, "When there is trust, there is the miracle of feeling oneself reflected in the energy of the other."[10]

Humans, on the other hand, are trained to shut down their hearts quite frequently, and we can be really mean and hurtful. That is never a concern when it comes to our animals. As children we all start out that way, but through exposure to modern culture and modern religions, we are conditioned to layer things over our hearts until by the time we are adults our hearts are fairly well suppressed. This quality of openheartedness, like the ability to communicate intuitively, can be relearned, and in this endeavor, animals are our best instructors.

What I see in my practice and in my own experience is that our animals are unrecognized healers and teachers for us, who bring us some of the greatest lessons and most profound healings we will experience in our lifetimes. They work seamlessly in the background, persisting over time; their teachings can be subtle, hidden, and almost invisible to us. They bring us the wisdom we need, and the healing necessary for our lives — we just have to look for it.

Roree and Lily

The best way to understand how our animals can help us heal through the process of mirroring is by telling a story about it.

Roree Severance called me about her cat, Lily, who was refusing to use the cat box and was urinating on her husband's possessions. I did an intuitive communication session with the cat, and she told

Roree and Lily

me that she wanted to focus on the relationship with Roree's husband and how he was interacting with Roree. Lily said he was being harsh to her and also to Roree; further, Roree was being unassertive, repressing her feelings and walking on eggshells around her husband. Lily said she didn't like him, he didn't like her, and she didn't think Roree liked him much either. Lily wanted me to talk to Roree about all this and maybe suggest to Roree that she take Lily and leave that house. To me it felt like Lily would not stop the inappropriate peeing until her concerns were met. Of course, I was reluctant to come out and say all this to Roree, so I beat around the bush until I realized that Roree was agreeing with everything I was suggesting, that is, everything I felt Lily had told me. At that point I told her my impressions from Lily, and I suggested a number of actions she could take for herself and for Lily to change the situation.

Months later I got an email from Roree reporting that everything I had shared with her was right on. She said she herself had started resorting to meanness and sarcasm in response to the situation, and she finally reached a point where she felt her husband would not change no matter what she said or did. When she realized this she began to distance herself emotionally from him. She also became more assertive, believing her point of view mattered and that she was capable, independent, and could make life safe for Lily. She made the corrections in the environment I had suggested — changing the litter and moving the cat boxes. She also asked her husband to be kinder to Lily and did a technique with him that I call "spirit talk," which involved talking to him in her imagination versus out loud (see chapter 7 for more on this).

Roree told me that everything had changed. At Roree's urging, her husband apologized to Lily and told the cat that he loved her; now he and Lily get along better. He jokingly asked Lily to use the cat box, and she started using it the next day and continued doing so consistently. Lily also "smiles" now when she lies in Roree's lap, and she has taken to sitting on Roree's husband's chest when he exercises in the morning. Roree reported that even the dogs are much more respectful to Lily. Roree realized that if she wouldn't put up with bad behavior from the other people in her life, why should she put up with it from her husband? Lily helped Roree by mirroring the dysfunction in her relationship with her husband. Mirroring can be like that — something that seems like an isolated issue with an animal can be about so much more. Animals help us heal by being our mirrors to show us when something is out of balance and not as it should be. Lily did this for Roree, unrelentingly. She must be grooming her whiskers over her phenomenal success in that venture.

How Animals Heal and Teach Us through Mirroring

Animals can sometimes alert us to medical problems directly, such as animals who are trained to sniff out cancer. Animals will also help us heal without being "asked." Through direct mirroring, they might sense and respond immediately when someone is about to have a seizure. Or their actions and behaviors might show us in more subtle, indirect ways something that is out of balance in our beliefs, relationships, or lifestyle. If we pay attention and honor their voices, our animals can help us identify our illnesses or unhealthy behaviors and help us go in new directions, as Lily did for Roree.

Because they stay tuned in to everything going on around them, and because of their deep compassion, animals are widely used in therapeutic settings. As I've mentioned, many therapists bring an animal into their sessions to help their clients. Horses are used in therapeutic riding schools to help individuals with many different issues, both physical and emotional. In the beautiful documentary *Horse Boy*,[11] a father enlists the aid of horses, nature, and shamanic healers in Mongolia on a quest to heal his son of autism. Animals are also constantly working to heal our closed hearts. Because they are able to make us feel so loved and safe, it allows us the freedom to open up again and begin healing old wounds. For this to work, however, you have to keep your heart open, pay attention to your animals, and receive the intuitive messages that come from your animals or from spirit. When you do that, you are journeying down your right path in life, and everything in your life begins to heal and change for the better.

What this means, in practical terms, is that any trauma or adversity that occurs with your animals, like dealing with a cat who won't cooperate, can be a form of communication on a deeper level. Beneath the surface, our animals could be presenting us with a particular challenge that we need to confront in our lives. Everything in our relationships with our animals, including their deaths, holds wisdom and healing for us. With every death of one of my animals, I learn more about my beliefs and expectation about death. Through the mirror of my reactions, my attitudes and feelings about death continue to change and evolve.

To see the lessons our animals bring to us we have to honor our intuition, which is not an easy task. I recall several lost animal cases where the clients had a strong sense that their animals were alive, but they had to persist in their search despite intense pessimism and discouraging comments from others. In one case a cat was mistaken as homeless and transported over fifty miles away to a new owner, who then negligently let the cat escape. When all this came to light, the woman who originally owned the cat was advised by friends and family to just give up. It was a hopeless situation: the cat could never find his way home from such completely foreign territory. But the woman followed her heart and pursued the search: she couldn't shake the belief that she could find the cat, and to give up would have been like giving up on herself. So she went door to door, paid to have postcard mailings in the area, and used my input for guidance about which areas to focus on. Against all odds, she found her cat.

Animals can teach us how to live in the moment, how to face our fear, how to trust, and how to love. Animals help us heal the damaged parts of ourselves, parts that are normally hidden from our view, by challenging us in ways that wake us up. In their interactions with us, our animals can even sometimes re-create old emotional wounds that need to be healed.

Tiffany and Butterfly

My friend Tiffany Faith's horse did this for her. Tiffany had purchased her Arabian mare, Butterfly, for her daughter, but soon discovered that Butterfly was not the calm, easy horse she had assumed. Instead, Butterfly was reactive and challenging every step of the way. In fact, she tried to walk all over Tiffany. To counter this, Tiffany had to learn techniques for setting boundaries, something she had not had to do with the other well-behaved horses in her life. She had to stop hand-feeding treats so Butterfly would not expect food at every encounter and get aggressive. Tiffany used natural horse training techniques (swinging a rope or waving a wand at the horse) to move Butterfly around in the pasture, to show Butterfly

Saige and Butterfly

how to maintain a respectful distance. Tiffany also moved the other horses in the pasture using these techniques as a way to take on the role, in a sense, of the top mare in the pasture. The top mare gets the respect.

In the process of working to get Butterfly to respect her and give her space, Tiffany realized that what Butterfly was doing was reminding her of her partner and how he was acting. Then she saw that throughout her life she had let people get in her space and push her around the way Butterfly was doing. She also realized that she could instead just say no to people the way she was doing with Butterfly. So she started setting boundaries with the people in her life and defining how she wanted them to act toward her.

Tiffany said it was funny to see Butterfly having a fit because she couldn't get her way, but not so funny to see the people in her life acting that way. Once she worked through the boundary issues with Butterfly, the horse became very calm and respectful and Tiffany could trust her to carry her daughter bareback using only a halter. Tiffany said she also permanently changed her interactions with other people, becoming very aware of the need to set and maintain proper boundaries. Ultimately, she learned to love and respect herself more because of the lessons from Butterfly.

Dickelle and Dakota

Some animals are clearly with their people to act in tandem with the person to help others heal. My friend Dickelle Fonda told me such a story about her husky, Dakota. Dickelle is a psychotherapist. When Dakota was alive, the dog helped her daily with her work. Dickelle says Dakota found her, not the other way around, and that she knows he was supposed to be with her. At the time, she didn't have dogs because her partner, Jevoid, didn't want any. But Dickelle realized, two years after having survived breast cancer, that she

Dickelle and Dakota

was not going to have any more children and she really wanted a dog. She finally convinced her partner to go along with the idea. While the couple was at their retreat cabin in Wisconsin, Dickelle idly checked through the paper and saw an ad for huskies from a local backyard breeder. She dismissed the idea and forgot about it, but on the way out of town at the gas station bulletin board, she saw the ad again, this time with a reduced price. Dickelle said she never looked at that bulletin board normally; she feels it was Dakota leading her to him. They called the breeder and went to see the puppies. Jevoid picked up a classic red-and-white puppy and Dickelle picked up a blue-eyed pup, but then a brown-eyed, black-and-white puppy latched on to her boot. He held on tight and would not let go. She picked him up, looked into his eyes, and had no choice. Dakota went home with them that day.

In the nearly twelve years that Dakota was part of her life, she came to know him as a soul mate, and he was a natural therapy dog. He was a healing force in the lives of many and brought a healing presence to her therapy office: he would sit at the feet of clients (who were open to dogs) and offer his head and deep brown eyes to those who were in distress, then he would settle again at their feet. He helped especially with trauma survivors. Dickelle recalled one woman who had been abused as a child. When she first came to Dickelle, she could not maintain eye contact and would look only at the floor; she could not accept love. Dakota used to lie at her feet. He would raise his head so she could pet and look at him and be soothed. Over the years this woman and Dakota formed a loving relationship. Years later the woman told Dickelle that Dakota was such a healer in her life that he helped her to begin accepting and giving love again.

Eventually, Dakota died of cancer in Dickelle's arms, but he managed to find his way back to that store where Dickelle had found the ad for huskies. When she returned a DVD to the store, she accidentally included a picture of Dakota in the envelope; it was taken

Dakota's Picture in Wisconsin Gas Station

in his later years showing him sitting in the snow and looking into the camera, right into the eyes of the viewer, as regal as ever. The woman in the store found the photo and posted it by the door. The next time Dickelle and Jevoid were there, the owner thanked them for the lovely picture of Dakota, not knowing he had died. When they learned of the story of how the picture got to them, the store owners had it framed, and it now graces the wall by the exit. People stop to admire Dakota daily and say hello to him. Dakota found his way back to his origins and to the place where he found Dickelle.

Animals and Enlightenment

I do believe that there is an element of fate or choice or purpose in all this — that on some level of spirit, unknown to us consciously, we choose our animals as our mirrors and they choose to come to us to serve us. Our animals are completely in sync with us; they know what we need. To learn from them is to gain admittance to a path leading to power and freedom. Ultimately, our animals help us reconnect to nature and to the harmony of being. Psychologist Margot Lasher says our animals teach us enlightenment. If enlightenment can be defined as being in the moment and connected to all, then animals live in enlightenment most of the time. Humans, Lasher points out, tend to do the opposite. We tend to focus on the future or past rather than the present, and on disharmonious emotions like fear and worry. One of the reasons people love animals so much is that being in the presence of an animal can bring you that instant feeling of harmony, calm, and timelessness.

As Margot Lasher writes:

Harmony is the normal, natural condition of the universe for animals. They do not live in fear; they do not live with an image of the world as dangerous. They do not have the human idea that some malevolent, evil spirit is out to get them. The world feels essentially safe and animals are essentially peaceful and happy.

Animals live in connection to their world. When something, even the smallest thing, begins to change, they stay aware. If the change brings a feeling that something is wrong, they listen to their feeling. Disharmony, at the level of feeling, is just this sense that something is wrong, that something is happening that doesn't belong. The animal separates itself from the part that doesn't belong. There is a disconnection between the animal and the world.

Staying connected is tuning into all feeling, including the sense that something is wrong. Staying connected means staying, as long as necessary, with awareness of separation and disharmony.

At exactly the right moment, the animal acts to restore harmony. This means acting to save itself, to save its babies, to save its companions, animal and human. It acts to restore a safe world for everyone.

Harmony at a personal level is the feeling of belonging. It is the sense of peacefulness when the energy inside you and the energy around you flow together. It is, ultimately, the sense of connection. Restoring harmony is returning to the peacefulness you feel when everything is connected. It is seeing the world again as a whole.

I think that humans feel the same flow between harmony and disharmony, but for some of us the proportions are reversed. A lot of the time we feel disharmony: stress, anxiety, something wrong. And then there are the moments of harmony, which in different spiritual traditions we call love, enlightenment, and pure awareness. I think that animals live most of their time in enlightenment.[12]

Exercise — Was Your Animal Your Teacher and Healer?

Think back over the animals you have had in your life, and your current ones. Are any of them obvious teachers and healers for you? In what ways?

Were any of them uncannily intelligent?

Did any of your animals do something to avert harm or save you or someone else?

Make a list of the animals in your life, past and present. Note down for each animal what was special and how that animal was your teacher and healer.

Share what you have written with a friend.

Positive Mirroring

Have you ever found yourself wishing you could be as happy, confident, or agile as your animal? Animals can act as role models for us. When we admire positive qualities in animals, it is no different than doing the same with the people in our lives. Animals can inspire us, give us hope and courage, and show us the positive side of life. They can show us something in themselves that we may want to mirror.

My cat Hazel was a positive role model for me. Hazel lived to be twenty-four. She died of kidney failure, but up until two weeks prior to that, you would not have been able to guess her age. She was healthy and frisky, loved rushing up tree trunks like a wild horse, and leapt to and fro on the railings of my front porch like a kid. When I first met her, Hazel marched right up to me, intent, I am convinced, on coming home with me. The moment I saw her I found myself saying automatically, "I want that cat." I encountered Hazel in an empty, trash-strewn lot while doing an environmental cleanup job down by the waterfront (in my previous occupation as an environmental scientist). She was about four, didn't belong to anyone, and hadn't really had a proper home. The people living by

Hazel

the waterfront knew her and told me she was feral, that she made the rounds to people's houseboats, and that she had had two litters of babies. Maybe it was because of her tough life, but you could just feel her confidence and power. Often I would say to her in jest, "Hazel, I want to be just like you when I grow up." I mimicked her self-confidence, her wit, her intelligence, and her commanding presence, or at least attempted to. I will never forget the positive influence she had on my life, day in and day out. Hazel was also my muse and helped me write my first two books.

What Animals Offer Us

We are attracted to animals for all kinds of positive qualities — their poise, their agility, their ability to love, their power and authenticity. When we seek to emulate them, we select a powerful template. Because animals are untouched by the ravages of modern culture, they offer us gifts that are often beyond what we can find through our relationships with people. Animals are experts at living in the moment, and when we are with them, we naturally slow down and become more present. Animals also love unconditionally and help us learn to do that by experiencing it from them. They are also much more attuned to the environment and teach us to be more alert and aware. Because they operate so much from the heart, they help us experience and learn what it means to be truly authentic. Animals through their behavior let us experience qualities like freedom, harmony, and peace that are hard to find in normal life.

Animals help us heal and grow spiritually. Because they forgive so easily, they teach us how to do that. With their companionship, we never have to feel alone, and because they are masters at playing and having fun, they help us have fun, too. It is largely through animals that humans are learning how to reconnect with nature and communicate intuitively. And every time we go through the death of an animal, we learn something new about the dying process.

Maryanne, Joey, and Java

When mirroring is completely positive, it tends to have an expanding positive effect. It is not often that both the human and animal sides of a relationship are totally positive, but that is what I see with my chiropractor.

Dr. Maryanne Kraft[1] works with both people and animals, and she and her two rat terriers, Joey and Java, are very healthy. They are all also athletic, enthusiastic, and just plain happy. Maryanne presents a positive role model for her human patients, and her dogs represent a positive role model for her animal patients. When you see a healthy, happy person or animal, it is just natural to want to know how they achieved that state. So by providing a healthy positive model, she and her dogs are encouraging others on the same path of health and wellness.

Maryanne and her dogs are not exactly like each other. She says that each dog represents a different part of her. If you have several

Maryanne, Java, and Joey (in lap)

animals, this will often be the case — each animal resonates and expresses a different aspect of you. Maryanne says that Java represents her quiet strength. Like her, he is also loyal and supportive, but when he wants his own time — time to himself — and you interrupt that, he can be reactive or show impatience. She said this is a mirror for her about her own behavior. When Java acts this way, she realizes this matches a quality in herself that she wants to modify and it helps her make a mental note to be more patient. Joey, on the other hand, expresses another side of Maryanne's personality: he is always easygoing, loving, and funny and nothing seems to bother him.

Margot and Hogahn

Margot Lasher sent me this story about mirroring, which she also told in her first book. It's about her dog Hogahn and dates back many years. She was on a walk with him on a narrow path in the woods of central Massachusetts. They often took this trail and rarely encountered anyone else, but that day, turning a bend, they came across a man and a large German shepherd standing just off the path. The man stood facing the dog and seemed to be in the middle of a training exercise.

When the man saw them, he tightened his dog's leash and screamed at Margot to put her dog on a leash. The shepherd had looked calmly at them at first, but then he picked up the man's panic and started pulling on the leash in their direction. Margot did not have a leash with her. The man seemed to have no relational connection to the dog at all; he was using brute strength and the metal prongs in the dog's neck to hold him. He was meanwhile screaming at Margot to "hold him."

Margot unthinkingly obeyed and grabbed Hogahn's collar. Hogahn was about ten feet from the shepherd and pulling just lightly on the collar. Hogahn was a large mixed-breed dog. There was no possibility that Margot could hold him if he chose to pull away, and she was feeling confused and frightened.

Margot and her current dog Shiro
(photo by Sylvia Ferry Smith)

At that moment Hogahn stopped, turned around, and looked at her. His turning required him to take his eyes off the shepherd; he looked at Margot pointedly, intensely. His turning was a real risk: he was taking his eyes off the danger in order to make contact with her.

Margo suddenly realized that she was acting as a stupid human in a conventional role, following the orders of an authority figure, in this case someone who had little understanding of his own dog.

She let go of the collar and Hogahn walked calmly past the shepherd with Margot following. The shepherd immediately calmed down. As she walked past the dog, she remembers feeling perfectly safe.

In that moment, when Hogahn turned to face her and she released his collar, she freed herself from a habit of obeying orders and assuming that the human had to be in control for things to come out safely. She saw her dog as an equal who did not have to be controlled. In fact, as a thinking being who was able to assess the situation, including the intentions of the other dog, Hogahn was more than equal.

In that same moment Hogahn saw her as someone who trusted him. He became the leader because he understood the situation better than she did. He stepped out of the usual dog role of either squaring off for a dog fight or obeying the leash-holder. She stepped out of the usual role of leash-holding human. They became a functioning, successful unit.

Carol and Dudley

Sometimes a negative experience can end up providing a positive mirror between human and animal. My colleague Carol Gurney[2] discovered a profound life lesson through a life-threatening situation with her horse.

One day Carol came home to find Dudley, her beloved Connemara horse, with a deep cut over his eye. She immediately realized this was beyond the care she could give him, so she called her vet, who came right over, gave Dudley a tranquilizer, then stitched the cut. All was going well until the vet gave Dudley a penicillin shot. Suddenly, to Carol's shock and horror, Dudley fell over backward and rolled down the hill behind her house until he crashed into the fence at the bottom. Now, we are talking about a thousand-pound horse who had totally lost control of his body. Neighbors came to the rescue and helped get Dudley freed from the fence, so

Carol and Dudley

that he was able to get up on his own. Dudley was now trembling, had blood pouring from his mouth, and his eyes were rolling back in his head. Carol was panicked he was going to die right in front of her. As the vet ran to her truck for supplies, she warned, "Carol, he's having a severe reaction to the penicillin. Don't go near him, he may flip over again, and you don't want to get in the way."

The only thing Carol could think to do was talk with him. Calling out to him, she said, over and over, "Dudley, breathe with me, stay with me." As Carol did this, she began to feel herself calm down, and she could sense Dudley focusing on her and linking to her. Then the miracle happened: Dudley heaved a huge sigh and lowered his head. Carol kept talking to him, and with each breath she took, Dudley's breathing calmed and started matching her rhythm. Now she felt it was safe to approach him, so she began stroking him, using the special massage technique called TTouch on his ears to help him feel calmer and release the trauma and shock he felt. His breathing continued to get calmer, and again he lowered his head and sighed.

The vet now felt it would be safe to walk him back up the hill to clean and hose off his legs, which were cut and scraped from crashing into the fence. Slowly, Carol helped Dudley up to the wash rack and turned on the water. Then Dudley panicked again, prancing and looking as if he would rear up and fall over backward once more! Carol still remembers her fear vividly: "This was it, I thought, now I really don't know what to do. Am I going to lose him?" Again, the only thing she could think to do was to talk with him. "Dudley," she said, "I am so scared and nervous right now because I don't know whether you are hurting somewhere and I can't hear you. I can't hear you, Dudley!" Carol's mind was racing: Should she try different types of bodywork? What could the vet do? Her horse was dying in front of her and she didn't know what to do. So she simply stopped thinking and talked with Dudley once again. "Dudley," she said, "I don't know what to do for you other than love you. All I can do is tell you I love you and ask you to stay with me." Closing her eyes, she concentrated on sending him love and feeling the close bond they had always shared. Then the miracle happened again: Dudley let out a huge sigh, dropped his head, and became quiet. Astonished, her vet turned to Carol and asked, "What happened? What did you do?" Carol answered simply, "All I did was tell him I loved him."

That day both Dudley and Carol had important lessons to learn. Dudley was a very strong and determined stallion, and he believed he needed to be in control of every aspect of his life. He most definitely did not want to trust or have to depend on a human. Going through that experience, being totally helpless and dependent on someone else, taught Dudley to trust. Carol had always felt love meant she had to be *doing*: taking care of someone, doing things for them, and having them do things for her. But that day Dudley taught her that love sometimes is simply *being there* for someone; not doing anything but just being there and loving them.

Dudley wasn't finished teaching Carol. As she became more

involved with her growing animal communication practice, she had less and less time to ride him. Dudley prided himself on his athletic abilities; being a working show horse was very important to him. One day, he asked Carol to let him go to another family who would be able to ride him and let him work. Although Carol had always felt committed to her animals for their lifetime, this time her lesson was twofold: She realized that animals have a right to live their life to their fullest potential. And also, even though it can be hard to do, sometimes, if you are unable to give them all they need, you have to love them enough to find them the perfect situation that fulfills their needs. So Carol let him go. She put the word out that Dudley needed a new home, and people started coming to see and ride him. Dudley wanted to choose his family, so each time Carol would ask him, "Is that the one?" Dudley kept saying no, until one day a very strong, skillful, twelve-year-old girl got on his back and was just thrilled. No matter what Dudley did, and he was very strong, she just laughed and loved him. "That's the one," Dudley told Carol. Today, Dudley is still with this same family and enjoying an active life in and out of the show ring.

Morgan and Scarlet

My friend Morgan Key told me that when she became pregnant with her daughter, she made the decision to hold up Scarlet, her friend's horse, as a positive mirror for herself. The mare was having a really easy pregnancy. As it progressed, Scarlet was active right up until the time her foal was born, and the birth went quickly and without complications. Meanwhile, Morgan's friends and acquaintances kept offering her the "helpful" advice that she should stop working early in her pregnancy; otherwise she would be miserable and possibly hurt the baby. They also informed her that, since it was a first birth, she was going to have a long, hard, painful labor. Morgan chose to ignore all that, instead deciding that she was going to have an easy pregnancy like Scarlet. Morgan has a horse barefoot

Morgan and Fallon

trimming business, which involves leaning over a horse's feet and cutting off excess hoof from the bottom and sides of each foot. It can be uncomfortable to do, and even if you are in the best of shape, it can give you a backache. Morgan kept working on horses up until the last three weeks of her pregnancy. She was fine the whole time, and her baby girl, Fallon, turned out to be an easy quick birth, just like Scarlet's.

Vonnie and Decon

Morgan told me another story, about her grandmother Vonnie Woodward, that is a perfect example of positive mirroring between an animal and a person. Vonnie is a very generous soul — she does a lot of volunteer work, and she would give you everything she has. She is always helping someone. Her cat Decon has taken on the same trait. Every morning he comes and finds Vonnie, at about the same time each day, and will meow, rub up against her, get in front of her feet, and do whatever it takes to make her go to the kitchen get some food, go outside, and feed the stray cats in the neighborhood. Then he just sits and watches as the stray cats get their free breakfast, basking in his altruistic gesture for the day. I'm sure he is frustrated that he can't get the food down and feed them himself.

Hanny and Gisela

Dr. Gisela Kenda is pediatrician in Austria. Her dog Hanny was a positive life teacher from the very beginning. Hanny was born with hip dysplasia in both hips, an abnormal formation of the hip socket; severe cases involve crippling lameness and painful arthritis in the joints. Even so, she had an irrepressible spirit and always just wanted to have fun. She really wanted to work and be useful and Gisela finally found the right avenue for Hanny in search-and-rescue work. The other competitors in her training group, and even her trainer, told Gisela to give up and not even try. Surely a disabled dog like Hanny would be doomed to fail, but Hanny and Gisela persevered. Gisela ended up training Hanny herself with the help of a friend. Through Hanny, Gisela developed her skill and became an

Gisela and Hanny

accomplished dog trainer. In 2005 Hanny competed in the Austrian champion search-and-rescue dog competition. The competition had three parts: searching and finding three to five people hiding in an area of about ten acres, obedience, and agility in an obstacle course. The search area was very steep and densely forested, but Hanny found all five hidden people in the search area in thirteen minutes, well under the twenty minutes allowed, which won her the championship in the search category. Hanny went on to participate in three world champion events and came in sixteenth in one of them.

Hanny showed Gisela how to go for what you want against all odds, while making sure that the goal was always to have fun. Hanny had some very unusual qualities. No dog dared to attack or do anything to Hanny; they always showed respect. When other dogs were aggressive or barking and coming toward her, she would stand still without moving, and the dogs would turn and go away. She would take the fear of dogs out of people, adults, and children. When people were afraid of her, she would move slowly toward them, and somehow they would forget their fear and pat her. This happened often. When Gisela had a problem, all she had to do was look at Hanny and the solution to her problem would pop into her head. She felt Hanny was sending this to her mentally. If Gisela was afraid of something, Hanny would sense it and go to her and calm her down.

When Hanny was eight, Gisela was able to afford to have two hip replacements done for her, and afterward Hanny lived the good life for another three and a half years. Hanny didn't want to get old. A year before she died she passed an exam in a new discipline — tracking. She was jogging about an hour in the mornings up until two weeks before her death. At that point she told Gisela intuitively, "Now my body cannot go anymore and it is better for me to leave." Gisela says Hanny's message to us is to be proud of your body, don't let yourself go, be active, and eat healthy.

Animals Know What We Need

Because they are always tuned in to us, our animals are keenly aware of what we need, and if they can help us, they will. When they do this to their detriment, we need to find some way to balance things out. But sometimes they help us in just the right way, with no adverse affect on themselves, which becomes a win-win situation. The following story is about one such animal who took it on herself to oversee her person's recovery from illness.

Carol and Luna

Carol Upton is a Canadian freelance writer and publicist. The story Carol shared with me shows how attuned our animals are to us, how concerned they are for our welfare, and how competent they are at helping us.[3]

On December 20, 2006, Carol was diagnosed with a rare form of head and neck cancer — adenoid cystic carcinoma, a malignant tumor, usually of the salivary gland, but in her case it had begun in the sinuses. The surgeon had removed enough of the tumor to

Carol and Luna

biopsy and to allow Carol to breathe, but the prognosis was not very good. Carol was going to have to visit an oncologist and undergo extensive treatment at the British Columbia Cancer Agency once the holidays were over. After that consultation, Carol said she and her partner walked back out onto the street in a daze that actually protected them from knowing too much too soon. They had no idea to what extent their lives had just been hijacked.

Suddenly, she felt like she had no past and no real future. Her mind wouldn't take her back to that nice safe place before the diagnosis, and it wouldn't take her too far ahead, either, because there might not be anything much up that road. Surgery was possible, but it was extensive and mutilating with no curative guarantees, and she decided against it. The alternative was six weeks of high-dose radiation and the hope of beating back the tumor. She made arrangements to leave her small hometown and live in Vancouver for the duration of daily treatment.

When she returned home, she was wearing a patch over one eye and could not see well enough to drive. She had lost weight, felt weak and tired, and the radiation burns to her face were painful. Her partner was working a great deal, and Carol was home alone for long periods of time. She had always found solace in nature, and she started seeing things in microcosm that she had not noticed before. Every flutter of a moth's wings seemed extraordinary now. The birds landing outside the office window appeared to be looking directly into her eyes. Her husky-Lab cross, Luna, was radiant as she rested near Carol's feet.

Every time Carol moved, Luna raised her head and searched Carol's face to see what was up. During this time Carol cried a lot, despairing that she would not survive this ordeal. When her tears fell, Luna was there to rest her chin on Carol's knee, gazing up steadily. Carol felt that Luna's eyes promised her that she and Luna could get through the process together. Slowly, some of Luna's shining confidence seeped into Carol's bones, and recovery seemed like a possibility.

Even though Carol's partner was walking Luna every day, Luna began poking Carol with her nose and herding her toward the door to get her moving. She and Luna began to take short walks down the street together, even though Carol couldn't see very well and felt unsteady on her feet. Previously, during walks, Luna had always galloped far ahead, but now she stayed close, looking back over her shoulder to be sure that Carol was still with her and waiting for Carol to catch up if she fell behind.

Carol said she knew that all animals had an amazing ability to heal, but she had never experienced it the way she did with Luna. In the world of animals, illness, injury, and even death are simply things that happen, and no other meaning is attached. She now understood that Luna saw her as an injured pack member who just had to get on her feet again; that wouldn't happen if Luna let Carol sit around. Like a typical human, Carol said she was thinking too much. Luna sent her a clear message that she needed to heal both body and spirit. Luna was determined to assist in every way she could, leading her down the street step-by-step so that she could grow strong again and comforting her when she needed to rest.

Carol says that today, she feels much more confident. Long, rambling walks with Luna and her newest rescue, Lucy, are the highlight of her day. To Carol's mind, her pack mate pulled her out of a dark and critical state; Carol says she wouldn't be where she is now without Luna's loving assistance.

Healing Is a Two-Way Street

Animals can learn positive qualities from us, just as we do from them. My animals have always been rescues. I was able to help Finnegan, my mini horse, by showing him a positive mirror of how people can be. He had been severely abused as part of a Mexican rodeo — ridden in a heavy western saddle by a heavy man. When

Marta and Finnegan

I got Finnegan, his feet were in horrible shape, and he had fat deposits all over due to metabolic syndrome (which includes symptoms of obesity and insulin resistance). He was terrified of people and would not let you get near him, particularly if you had a rope. He would kick out at you if you got close, and when he had his feet trimmed, he would rear, bite, and buck the whole time. I had to leave his halter on for the first two months, as that was the only way I could catch him, and I had to trap him in a paddock and chase him around at that.

Part of my strategy with him was to talk out loud and keep reminding him he was safe, had a new home for life, and would never be hurt again. I also asked my other horses to help Finnegan learn to trust me and other people. After locking him in the paddock, I would sit with him, reading a book and ignoring him, so he would not feel any pressure from me, but I had a bucket of cut-up carrots and apples at my feet to make me interesting. The treats finally did the trick. He started coming up to me as I sat reading in the paddock. I would give him a treat and let him leave. After a few days of that, I started grabbing his harness at the same time as giving the treat, then I would scratch him and let him leave. The next stage was putting the rope over his neck while holding the harness and giving lots of treats. By doing this process repeatedly over a few months, I finally got to the point where I could walk up to him with a treat, and he would stand still while I put on a halter or fly mask. I also fed him treats nonstop while he was getting his feet trimmed to get him to stop biting, kicking, and rearing.

It took a while to turn the corner, but now Finnegan is lovable, lets me approach easily, and is calm for trimming. I switched him to a low-carbohydrate diet, and he has lost his crestiness and fat deposits, and his feet are much better. I don't have to chase him anymore, and he likes to give me kisses now, though sometimes he thinks it is fun to turn it into a nip at the last minute. I provided a positive model of trust, fairness, and respect for him to follow.

In general, our positive mirroring for rescue animals can be that we help them emotionally, help them achieve some spiritual dream or goal, give them the freedom to excel mentally, or pave the road to their physical recovery. Good rescue groups and individuals do this by restoring trust, building confidence, providing physical support, giving love, and finding the animal the right home to thrive in.

Prison Programs and Second Chances

In another situation of mutual positive mirroring, prison programs now exist all over the United States and internationally where inmates receive training to help homeless shelter dogs. The prisoners learn from the mirror of the dogs in their charge to be compassionate and joyful and to feel a sense of worth and responsibility. They also gain skills that can help them find a job. The dogs, who might otherwise have been killed, are helped to overcome their fears, aggressive tendencies, and lack of self-confidence; they are made more adoptable and given a second chance.

The prisoners train dogs for all kinds of purposes, as assistance guide dogs, to help disabled veterans or those with post-traumatic distress, and for jobs in security (drug sniffing, bomb sniffing at airports, and so on). The staff at the prisons report that the programs make inmates more friendly toward one another, and recidivism rates for the inmates in these programs are very low.

Similar programs allow prisoners to train and rehabilitate horses and learn horse management skills that they can use to find a job when released. In an article about a program for women inmates in Florida,[4] one inmate commented that for nine hours a day she can be happy and nurturing, have an opinion, and enjoy something she loves. Even though she is incarcerated, because of the horses, she feels free. Another woman commented that the horses give her unconditional love and unbelievable trust and make it possible to believe in the future again. The horses benefit by getting more fit, better behaved, and more adoptable, so they have a chance of finding a second home rather than being sent for slaughter, which is what happens to most retired racehorses. The parallels in their circumstances — in which both inmates and horses live at the margins of society and, in different ways, are at risk of being discarded — are certainly apparent to the women when they enter the horse rehabilitation program. It is amazing that by being around the open and loving nature of the horses, these women are able to come out of their inner prisons and feel love, joy, and self-confidence in the midst of what would otherwise be the shattering experience of incarceration.

Animals Can Mirror Our Dreams

I didn't realize it when I got Rio, the gray Arabian in the photo with me on the back of the book, that he would be my dream horse, but he turned out to be. When I saved him, I thought he was dying, and my plan was to give him a nicer place to die than where I had found him. Instead, he got healthier and healthier until he was fit to ride. Then I found out that he had been an endurance horse. I had just lost my trail horse, Dylan, and I didn't think I would find another horse I felt safe riding, but Rio filled that bill and more. He turned out to be a bombproof trail horse who loved to go on adventures. I could not have found a better match if I had gone out looking, but I didn't find him, he found me. Rio is gone now; he died in his late twenties. I told him many times in the years I had him how grateful

I was that he brought me my dream. Riding Rio in the mountains, at the beach, and on the trails has made for some of the happiest times of my life.

Joyce and Dan

Joyce Geier, a top-level international sheepdog competitor, found her dream mirrored back to her in the form of a tiny puppy. She was at a sheepdog trial in the United Kingdom competing with two of her dogs, and a good friend of hers from Ireland was judging. He mentioned that a mutual friend had a litter of pups that Joyce might be interested in: the mother was the same as one of Joyce's good (and favorite) dogs, and the father was very closely related to Joyce's number one, world-team, top-class dog. For some reason, Joyce found herself asking if the litter was all spoken for, commenting that with that pedigree, the pups were bound to be outstanding. Her friend responded that there was a dog pup and a bitch pup left. Joyce said that some voice other than her own said, "Not now there isn't. You can pick one for me and send it over to the States."

Joyce's friend decided to import the other pup, and about five weeks later, Dan and his litter sister, Chevy, arrived in Newark Airport. Joyce and her friend went to pick up both pups, who had traveled quite well. They drove the pups back to

Joyce and Dan

Joyce's house, gave them water and a snack, and let them run in the yard. Like any good pups, they were absolutely full of energy and tearing about, exploring and playing and just generally being little terrors.

While Joyce was watching this, she thought to herself, "What on earth was I thinking? I need a puppy like a hole in the head!"

No sooner had she thought that than Dan skidded to a stop, turned, and looked her straight in the eye, and a little voice in Joyce's head said, "I am the dog you've been looking for."

Then Dan promptly resumed gallivanting and jumped straight into the baby wading pool with his sister, tumbling head over heels on top of her. Joyce said she didn't know that she was looking for another dog, but there he was. She says he is by far one of the nicest pups she has ever raised in her thirty-plus years of experience with sheepdogs.

She found out that he was a mirror for her hidden dreams when she attended a workshop I taught in Vermont. On the first day the participants learned how to do the basics of animal communication. The second day I covered the subject of how our animals are our teachers and healers. I had people match up in pairs and interview each other's animals, intuitively, about various issues, one being what the animal felt his or her purpose was in the person's life. Joyce had not told us anything about how she got Dan; all we knew was what we saw at the class, a really happy, goofy puppy, zooming around and enjoying life. Joyce's partner for the exercise was Kinna, a woman who also had Border collies and had studied sheepherding work — further proof that there are no accidents. Or at least, a lot of the time some hidden force seems to be at work in our lives. Kinna only knew that Joyce planned to train Dan to be a sheepherding dog. Here is what Kinna wrote when she asked Dan about his purpose in Joyce's life.

> I definitely need to be in her life! No question! We are going to go incredible places together! All the Border collies sent

me to Joyce! They are really supportive of how she works and what she can show the world! I am an ambassador for them. Joyce is going to teach me new things that no other Border collie out there has been taught. I'm going to be her experiment dog. I'm going to learn so much! The Border collies of the world have been waiting for someone like her. They chose me to do this!!!!!

Halfway into the exercise, Kinna called me over and asked me, "Can you get an animal who talks all in exclamation points?" I laughed and assured her it was possible. After hearing what Kinna believed that Dan had said to her intuitively, Joyce told us that for some time she had thought that she was going to do something different and new in the world of sheepdog trials. She didn't have a clue what it was going to be; she just felt certain that she was going to do it. When Dan came into her life, she knew that he was the dog with whom she would embark on this new venture. Dan is still a puppy, so the journey has just begun. We don't know where it will lead, but Dan is the mirror for the hidden dream Joyce has for doing something completely different in her field.

Exercise: Positive Mirroring

Who are the animals in your life who you feel are now or have been positive mirrors for you?

List each animal and describe what that animal is doing or has done for you that no one else could have given you.

If the animal has died, describe how you are still being affected in a positive way in your life by that animal.

Negative Mirroring

Negative mirroring is the major focus of this book because in this type of mirroring an animal may be misbehaving or doing something negative that we want to change and improve. The following story is an unusual example of this.

There is a radio station in my area that plays comedy all day long, and I love to listen to it when I have time. Without comedy I think I would have gone a bit crazy by now. One day comedian Jeff Dunham was featured, and he told the perfect story about negative mirroring. He started out by saying that his skit was a true story, which I believe. He said his wife loves Chihuahuas and had a female Chihuahua that she wanted to breed. They rescued a stud male Chihuahua, who was half the size of their female (Jeff: "How you can call anything a stud that weighs two and a half pounds?"), with whom the male sired three puppies. The couple kept the runt of the litter, who was one and a half pounds. For some reason the runt decided that his two best friends in life were Jeff and the family's Great Dane. The little runt liked Jeff so much that when Jeff and his wife would go to bed mad at each other, not having made up yet after a fight, the runt would sneak over to the wife's side of the bed and pee on her in the middle of the night.

Being an animal communicator, I get calls daily about cats peeing outside the box, dogs peeing on the rugs, cats spraying in the house, even cats peeing on the bed, but never about a dog peeing on a spouse to make a statement. That story is really the ultimate pee story, and it's instructive because anyone can see what's going on.

Usually, by the time people contact an animal communicator about an animal's inappropriate elimination, they are at their wits' end. The cause of the problem isn't obvious; they have "tried everything" and are angry, upset, and frustrated. Their question is always, why would a cat or dog have this behavior? There is no simple answer except to say that, since most people can't hear intuitive communication, animals have to find some other way to get a message across to us. One way is by acting out, which can take many forms. In the case of improper elimination in cats, the message could be something direct and straightforward like, "Hey, I don't like the kind of litter you are using, and while you're at it, get a different kind of cat box and move it somewhere more private." Step one is often to reconfigure the box and contents and see if that solves the problem. Or the animal could be saying, "I am sick, and I have a physical problem." Often a trip to the veterinarian to check for a bladder infection will help with the immediate problem. But then, one should ask, why did a bladder infection arise in the first place? Following that trail can lead to causes like too much stress in the house, poor food, or immune system issues caused by the kind of care the animal is receiving.[1] Those causes, in turn, could also contain elements of mirroring related to the humans in that animal's life.

To identify whether there are issues related to mirroring at play, I ask the animal and also get a sense intuitively of whether there is mirroring and what it could be about. Depending on what information I get from that process, I might ask the person, for example, if he or she is under a lot of stress, or not eating well, or experiencing a poor immune system due to unhealthy living habits. If the answer is yes, then we might look at whether the animal, by getting ill, is trying to tell the person about a problem the person has. This single act — an animal getting ill and, in so doing, forcing the owner to change and grow — happens so often, in such varied ways, and with such obvious intention, that I have given the topic its own chapter (the next one, "In Sickness and in Health").

In this chapter I discuss all the other ways an animal can act out to make a statement and what kind of mirroring this can reflect. For example, when an animal does something annoying, it could really be a message; an animal usually isn't being bad for no reason. Of course, the behavioral message may not reflect mirroring; it could just be an animal expressing its own emotion, like saying, "I'm angry and you need to change how I am being treated." An example would be a dog who becomes aggressive in response to mistreatment by young children.

But like Jeff Dunham's Chihuahua, the animal's behavior could also be mirroring something in us that is not in balance and that needs to change. It could be something about our lives, our relationships, or our beliefs. Invariably, when mirroring happens, animals act out to show us what we don't want to look at, fears and issues we are probably avoiding, in order to help us to see clearly what we need to change to create more happiness and harmony in our lives. That Chihuahua was simply acting like the couple's one-and-a-half-pound marriage counselor.

Mirroring Is Ubiquitous, Common, and Unavoidable

In theory, the best way to avoid having your animal act out is to learn how to communicate intuitively with your animal and check with your animal every day to make sure that all is well, and then to follow up on every complaint in order to make sure your animal is happy at all times. Well, even I don't do that! And yes, my animals have acted out. From my perspective, there is no way to avoid having your animal act out at some point or other. This is because they can't tell us what is wrong in a straightforward manner, and inevitably something will always go wrong. Life is not perfect. It's also because they can't leave a situation if something is bothering them, like we can. Domestic animals are, for all intents and purposes, our prisoners. We can give them a really nice prison, but unless they are completely free to leave, which does apply to many cats, they are tied to our lives inextricably. Everything that throws us off throws our animals off. Our animals experience our imbalances as if the imbalances were their own. In acting out, all they really want to do is heal everything and everyone, so that there can be peace and happiness.

You don't need a degree in animal communication to be able to sense when your animal is unhappy or when something is wrong; you just need to pay attention. However, animals are often subtle about their problems; as a survival technique, they don't go around broadcasting their vulnerabilities. So pay attention to any slight change in behavior — this could signal a hidden problem. Also pay attention to how you feel and what thoughts go through your head. People will often dismiss thoughts and feelings they have about their animals as a fanciful imagination or "just worrying." It's better to take these incidents seriously. Follow up on it if you think your animal might be getting ill or might be unhappy about something. Don't just ignore it.

Not only is mirroring common (though often hard to detect), and unavoidable, it is also not about blame. You cannot let yourself feel guilty about mirroring — that's not the point. The point is to understand it and thereby transform a negative or potentially negative situation. One of the psychologists I interviewed for this book, Jay Rice, pointed out that, for whatever reasons, modern culture encourages people to feel like they are wrong and bad if they get sick or if their life is not going perfectly. He suggests that this approach needs to be reframed and reconsidered: when you are dealing with illness or some life problem, consider it instead an opportunity. A bad experience in life will be either your teacher or your tyrant. If you can accept it without blame, you will learn from it. Then, by stopping and evaluating what led to the problem, you can make necessary, positive changes in your life. Without that apparently negative experience, you would not have had the opportunity to heal, to become happier, and to be more in balance. So mirroring is, in essence, the gift our animals give us. When we can learn from their gift, we are always better for it.

My colleague Carol Gurney is a pioneer in animal communication and was the first in the field to recognize and develop the concept of mirroring between animals and people. Carol has worked with thousands of clients, and she has lectured and taught about animal communication, including mirroring, for more than twenty-five years. Carol knows the concept of mirroring can be difficult for people to fully understand. When Carol explains to people that their animal is most likely mirroring them, people often feel guilty, thinking it is their fault that their animal is becoming ill or behaving badly. Instead, Carol says, it is important for people to understand that their animal is actually trying to help them by showing them an aspect of themselves that they need to address. It is also very important to understand that this is a process: once you observe that your animal is mirroring, then you must ask yourself questions and get to the root of the issue. What is being reflected or mirrored? Then, once this is determined, you have to figure out what actions to take to solve the problem that led to the mirroring.

Carol believes, as do I, that animals often, if not always, make a conscious choice to mirror their person's behavior or situation in order to help the person. Animals are in a wonderful position to help people work through their issues. We are better able to accept lessons that come from love, and we know that our animals' love is unconditional. Animals are often in our lives to be our healers and our teachers; this is their gift to us.

It is important to recognize that when your animal is mirroring, he or she usually cannot stop until *you* acknowledge your animal's behavior and make changes in yourself. Animals can't change in a vacuum; their people have to help them make the changes. So while it may be the animal's choice to mirror us, it is our responsibility to be accountable for ourselves and to handle our own emotions and issues so that our animals can let go of the mirroring.

Carol says that if you search for it, you will often see an aspect of yourself in each one of your animals. You may not like what you see at times, but what a great way to learn about yourself. She says that it can sometimes be the greatest therapy you can hope to have. Her advice, if you see something being reflected for you, is to thank your animal for showing you this part of yourself. This gratefulness is encouraged, she says, if we hold the attitude that our animals are not showing us that something is *wrong* with us, but they are simply showing us parts of ourselves that need to be nurtured. She says it is important to ask your animal to let go of the mirroring so that you can learn the lesson for yourself. Animals really need to know that you are taking over and that they have empowered you to do so, otherwise you won't learn this great lesson of love.

Also, remember, animals can mirror our positive as well as negative aspects; it all furthers our spiritual growth. Carol has learned to see all her animals as barometers of herself, observing how they can shift and change to reflect changes in her life. You can see this, too, if you observe your animals closely. Carol says it is interesting to observe how things go when you bring a new animal into your life. As you watch their behaviors improve, it's a reflection of you and things getting better for you. Look at what you bring in. Do you have happy animals? Complex animals? Figure out why.

Carol learned about how animals reflect us by first seeing it in her animal clients. When she spoke intuitively with the animals, if they could not explain what was going on or tell her why they were behaving in a certain way, then in those cases, there was often a mirroring situation.

Carol believes one of the primary reasons animals are in our lives is to teach us how to love ourselves the way they do — unconditionally. She believes animals are some of the best teachers and role models we have because they provide a safe environment for us in which to learn. She told me the following story about one of the first times she applied the concept of mirroring to herself. It's a story about a Border collie, Jessie, whom she had years ago when she first started out in the field of animal communication.

Jessie and Carol

Behind Carol's house is a wonderful, open park area far away from any roads where she used to take Jessie and let her run off-leash. But Carol found that when she turned Jessie loose, Jessie would not come back immediately when Carol called her; instead she would

Carol and Jessie

run and run until *she* felt like coming back. Obviously, Jessie really enjoyed these times; she acted so carefree and happy. But Carol increasingly didn't enjoy them; in fact, each time she called and called for Jessie, she could feel herself becoming angrier. Carol remembers asking herself, "Why won't she come when I call? Obedience is so important, isn't it?" Then one day, she felt her anger become rage, and this stopped her in her tracks. "What is going on?" she asked herself. "Why am I becoming enraged?" As she thought it over, she tried to remember what situation Jessie might be showing, or mirroring for, her. She asked herself, "What am I so angry about, really? Is it about Jessie not obeying or about her feeling so carefree and happy? Am I actually jealous of Jessie?"

Carol thought back to her childhood, a time when she was not permitted to express her emotions freely. Schooled by stern Catholic nuns, she was quickly suppressed any time she got out of line, disobeyed, or showed any independence. She was never allowed to just run, free and happy. Obedience to someone else's rules was all she was permitted. Now, she realized, watching Jessie run so free and happy made her envious that she didn't have that in her life. But why didn't she? No one stood in her way anymore. As an adult, the only person stopping her from being a free spirit was herself. Just as Jessie showed her, Carol could be free and happy, too.

This realization spurred some major changes in Carol's life. Her social and personal life changed as she recognized ways she could set herself free. She allowed herself to take the dance lessons she had always desired. She got a bicycle and took long rides on country roads. When she gave herself the freedom to do things she enjoyed, when she allowed herself to be much more relaxed and less structured, she also found her attitude toward Jessie shifting. Was it really so very important that Jessie instantly obey every command? With Carol's change in perspective, Jessie could relax. And guess who started coming back when she was called?

Negative Mirroring and Psychodrama

The most basic form of negative mirroring is the direct response of an animal to a person in the moment, for example, a dog who slinks away and hides when people start arguing. Such behaviors are easy to interpret. This type of observation of minute physical reactions and expression is the backbone of horse-therapy programs. Horses, through their behavior, mirror the feelings and thoughts of the participants in the therapy programs, allowing these people to see aspects of themselves, reflected in the horse's behavior, that they may have been unable to see in normal life or were unconscious of. Thus, a fearful person can create fear and tension in the horse, which the horse will express by becoming restless and reactive.

Horse expert Tina Hutton says that if a person is uptight or upset, the horse won't be able to ignore this. The horse will read the emotion and must react to it. Horses often respond either by getting anxious or shutting down, but they will find some way to express their reaction. For instance, when a person works hard all day sitting at a computer and then rushes over to the stable to ride, a situation is unknowingly created where the horse will mirror this person's stress. Then the stress is compounded when, in the interest of saving time, the person rushes through the stages of preparation — haltering the horse quickly, leading the horse without focus or balance, grooming quickly, and saddling and bridling quickly. Then, while riding, if the horse moves too quickly, is nervous and spooky, or simply lacks focus, the rider gets very frustrated, not re-alizing what created these behaviors. Tina says that if riders want their horses to move with fluidity and balance, they have to con-sider the impact of their own physical conditions and patterns.

When negative mirroring is indirect, it is harder to spot, and it falls into a category I have termed "psychodrama." This type of mirroring involves an animal and a person acting out or re-creating some unresolved issue from the past. This usually has to do with a deep-seated belief or emotional trauma. I believe that people can unconsciously seek out certain animals and situations in order to re-create a painful experience or condition as a way to heal from the associated trauma they still retain. Psychologist Margot Lasher agrees that this can happen. She said psychologists and psychiatrists in the field of post-traumatic stress disorder are exploring the idea that when the context around you is similar to some past trauma, you experience the same emotions as felt in the original trauma. Lasher also said that cognitive psychologists are examining the possibility that it is not the events that happen to you in life that are significant, but rather how you experience and relate to them. In a way, this is similar to the notion that you create your own reality. My theory is that animals enter our lives, either by finding us or by us finding them, in order to help us actively recapitulate a trauma and do just that kind of healing. But I couldn't find any formal discussion of this premise in the field of psychology or psychiatry. Equine-assisted learning practitioner Dr. Beverley Kane says that animals can choose to take on and dramatize our issues for a variety of reasons. As Tinkerbell, the guardian fairy, did for Peter Pan, our animals are sometimes willing to drink the poison by taking on our pain or dysfunction, even our physical illness, to help us thrive. Unlike Tinkerbell and Peter, however, you and your animal can have a happy ending. If you work to correct a negative mirroring situation, you can bring both yourself and your animal to a better, healthier existence. You will read many stories in this chapter and the next about animals and people doing exactly that.

Negative Mirroring Stories

The following series of stories from my clients and students will give you a feeling for how negative mirroring works, what to look for to detect it, and how it has led to growth, breakthroughs, and good outcomes in a variety of situations. It's somewhat easy to see mirroring when it's happening between other people and their animals, but much harder to see in yourself with your own animal. That's why the situation can persist for some time before you begin to perceive that something deeper could be happening. This was the case for my student Rebecca Trono.

Rebecca's Stories

Rebecca and her husband live with a Shih Tzu–terrier mix named Emmett. Ever since he was a puppy, regardless of their best efforts, he always displayed misplaced aggression, attacking the couple's other dog, Buster, whenever there was the slightest unexpected noise or stressor of any kind.

Rebecca told me it wasn't until she attended one of my workshops that she saw that Emmett was mirroring her own behavior. Rebecca realized that when she experienced stress, she would at times turn on her husband, becoming short-tempered and sometimes lashing out at him. Seeing this connection between herself and Emmett helped her to modify her behavior with her husband.

Rebecca and Emmett

One of Rebecca's previous dogs, Tedi, mirrored Rebecca's husband completely. Tedi, a Shih Tzu, was the love of their lives, being the most affectionate, sweet dog either of them had ever known. The only thing that concerned Rebecca about him was that he was so mild-mannered that when he was attacked or threatened, he did nothing about it — just didn't respond. This personality trait was very much like Rebecca's husband, who is kind, gentle, sweet, and easygoing to a fault — traits that, when they had Tedi, were causing some real issues and challenges in the couple's relationship.

Tedi had a few instances of being attacked by another dog. One huge shepherd mix would pick him up and shake him like a rag doll, slamming him down on the pavement. Tedi didn't respond and didn't try to run away (which may actually have been a physiological response). He always came out of it okay, but Rebecca was struck by Tedi's passivity.

Then one afternoon, after a particularly upsetting discussion, Rebecca and her husband parted to different areas of the house. Rebecca was fuming. In a little while, she walked into the kitchen. From there she could see her husband, lying on the sofa in the living room. On his chest was little Tedi. Her heart melted to see this man, well over six feet tall, very much a *guy*, spending what he called "chest time" with his favorite boy. Rebecca later told Tedi that he saved her marriage because she was able to see past her frustration to the real strength of someone who can walk away from confrontation, one who consciously chooses peace over anger and hurt. Tedi and her husband were two peas in a pod, and Tedi helped Rebecca see the blessings in their personalities.

Linda and Clipper

Linda Allen's story is one that is probably repeated daily by thousands of animals who are taking on and acting out our emotions as quickly as we can suppress them. When Linda and her husband recently sent their twenty-year-old daughter to college in Europe

Linda and Clipper

for a year, Linda told herself everything was fine and that this would be a good opportunity for her daughter. The couple had plans to visit their daughter during the year, so all was well. But their dog, Clipper, wasn't fine. Normally calm and cheerful, he became agitated, barked at people and animals from the window, got rough when playing with other dogs, and started jumping up on furniture and people. Linda thought he was just missing their daughter and acting out. Then one day she recognized her own behavior in Clipper's. On the surface, she was telling herself she was fine, but underneath she felt like a nervous wreck, worrying about whether her daughter was safe, healthy, able to find good food and make new friends. Linda said she found herself pacing around the house, unable to fall asleep, and randomly snapping at her husband. Right before she attended my beginning workshop, Linda realized that Clipper had been mirroring her. In the workshop she learned how to talk to Clipper and get messages back from him. She explained to Clipper that he didn't need to mirror her stress anymore. Linda stays in touch with her daughter, so she can be calmer and more confident that her daughter is doing well. As a result, Clipper and Linda have both relaxed — and now he mirrors a happier person.

Angus and Su

Su Wickersham is a professional animal communicator.[2] Her dog, Angus, like her, is sensitive, and both are very empathetic. Angus is also very expressive, and you can tell when he is pouting; Su thinks she pouts, too. They both get over things quickly, though. Angus

Su and Angus

is friendly to just about everyone, but he will hold a grudge, or rather hold back affection, if he thinks he's been ignored. Su realized recently she was doing that to her sister. It was hard to admit, but she could see that she had been withholding herself because of some life choices her sister has made that Su didn't approve of. Su then noticed that when her sister came to visit, Angus was mad and wouldn't go over to see her like he normally did. Su felt that way, too, though out of politeness she didn't act it out. Angus was doing it for her. Another mirror between herself and Angus is that, when he is upset, he gets withdrawn and becomes quiet and noncommunicative, and so does she.

Joni and Rascal

Often what negative mirroring shows us about ourselves relates to things that have happened in childhood, that we have forgotten or suppressed, but that still affect us. That is what artist and horse-woman Joni McKim[3] discovered in her situation with her horses. Joni is skilled at barrel racing, which is a timed sport that involves racing around a series of barrels. She and her daughter compete at the top level in barrel racing circles. Joni and I have had a few sessions together, and I am helping her be more successful by steering her in the direction of natural care for her horses. Well over three years ago, she removed the horseshoes from her barrel racing horses and went barefoot with her horses, and she has seen a big improvement in their level of comfort, flexibility, and speed. She also switched over to using treeless saddles, saddles that are more flexible and lightweight, and her horses are more comfortable and responsive. More recently, Joni called about a different problem. When she rode her horse, she was just flopping around and felt she was "riding like a grandma." Joni said she had lost her nerve, and she had no idea why. The way Joni described it to me, she was frozen in fear and felt as if she was being betrayed by her own body.

Joni and Rascal (photo by PixelWorx)

I got some intuitive impressions that I checked out with Joni, and in our discussion she realized that her issue stemmed from past experiences she had with her mother and her sister. When growing up, there had been a lot of competition, and Joni had always deferred to her mother and sister. In addition, Joni felt she had not really been supported in any way in childhood, so she was dealing with a lot from the past. Somehow the fact that her daughter was competing in the same field had brought back all that old pain, and Joni was falling into the childhood pattern of giving up, deferring, and devaluing herself. I suggested that she and her daughter have a long talk and come up with some agreement about supporting each other and never making any disparaging comments.

Joni said she and her daughter talked for four hours, came up with their agreements, and they were off. Everything cleared up for Joni immediately because she could see how it was all related to a past that she didn't need to hold on to. With that her riding immediately improved. The horses, who had just been holding the space for her, took off and started to excel. Joni said in a recent competition she and her daughter came in ninth and tenth. Not shabby. I told her if she gets up to the winners' circle with the rhinestones and the photo ops, she has to fly me in.

Kati and Vilmos

I have a soft spot in my heart for Vilmos, not to mention that he has a wonderful name. Vilmos, through acting out, led Kati Gabor on a path she might not otherwise have taken. I'm so glad he did, as Kati is embarked on an education project to teach children and adults to reconnect with nature using intuitive communication.[4]

She adopted Vilmos (then named Sylvester) from the local animal shelter in Ottawa. He was everyone's favorite cat at the shelter, and he walked into her family's life with such grace and dignity that they had to rename him Sir William (or "Vilmos" in Hungarian, which is Kati's mother tongue). The family was blessed by

Kati and Vilmos

Vilmos's company for about a year, when one summer day he didn't return from his nightly adventures. They looked everywhere for him and did everything they could to find him, but they found no trace of him. Eventually they gave up the search and assumed he had been killed somehow.

A year or so later, feeling Vilmos was well and truly gone, the family adopted two young cats, littermates from the shelter, naming them Tiger and Panther. A few months after they had adopted the new cats, Kati received a call from the Toronto animal shelter. They asked whether she could come and pick up her cat. She was stunned: Ottawa and Toronto are separated by about two hundred twenty miles. Vilmos had disappeared over a year ago, and now she found out he was still alive. Two days later she picked him up because "by coincidence" she happened to have a conference in Toronto, for which she was scheduled to leave the day after the phone call. The shelter that had picked up Vilmos from the street was able to identify him by the chip implant he carried. When Kati got Vilmos back home, he strolled in as if nothing had changed. His dominance was never questioned for a moment, and the cats all befriended each other in a few days.

Sir William — the "princely fugitive" — still likes to escape whenever he gets a chance. One of his disappearances prompted Kati to contact me for help in locating him. Kati says that Vilmos and I brought her to the realization that communicating with animals is "for real" and that she has her part to play in it. After this incident, they fortified their fence and made it virtually escape-proof. Whenever Vilmos occasionally finds his way out through the door or gate, they find him more quickly each time. Kati is now adept at animal communication, so she and Vilmos can communicate when he is lost. Kati can see now that he only tries to go away when the people around him are not present for him or for themselves, with no time to play, no time to sleep, no time to meditate, and no time to connect with each other. Vilmos, Panther, and Tiger know what kind of life is worth living, and they are holding that mirror for Kati and her family.

Cecilia and Akasha

Cecilia Götherström and her husband had Akasha, their Siberian husky, for a bit over a year when the dog began acting out quite a lot. One of the things the dog started doing was running off far away — as far as the next suburb. Even though husky books and trainers said huskies could not be off-leash, quite a few of the dogs

Cecilia and Akasha

from Akasha's breeder could be off-leash, and up until that point, Akasha had been fine off-leash. Cecilia had the feeling that this behavior had nothing to do with Akasha being a husky, but with certain needs not being met.

Cecilia went to an animal communicator, my colleague Gerrie Huijts, to try to get at what might be going on. Gerrie told Cecilia that Akasha wanted Cecilia to change her life so that it was more comfortable and more accurately reflected who she was. Gerrie told Cecilia that she felt Akasha wanted Cecilia to live her own life and not adjust to everyone and everything around her. Cecilia felt these messages from Akasha mirrored the way Cecilia felt daily about her job. At the time she was working for a multinational corporation. She was highly regarded for her ability to adapt and excel in the corporate world, but she had also had three incidents of burnout. Cecilia had to come to terms with the fact that this position was not right for her

As soon as Cecilia and Akasha started spending more time together in nature — mushing, biking, running, hiking, and walking on the beach — not only did Akasha's behavior change but Cecilia got all the inspiration she needed to change her occupation and follow her chosen path as a professional animal communicator. On this path, Akasha is not only Cecilia's guide, but also her companion and best friend.

Cecilia says it can still take her about a day to realize when she gets off balance and off track. Akasha will tell her by acting up when they take a walk, pulling the leash as if she were an elephant, first this way, then that way. Akasha might refuse to walk and sit down, or she'll walk in the opposite direction, or she'll suddenly run and tug Cecilia across the street. Cecilia said, when she gets to the point of frustration and asks, "What do *you* want?" Akasha smirks and sends her the message back intuitively, "Well, what do you want? You are all over the place and not where you are supposed to be!" Every time Akasha does this, she helps bring Cecilia back to where she should be. Sometimes Akasha does this in a harsh way, if Cecilia is too closed and "stuck in life" and cannot listen to the "whispers" from Akasha, or it can be in a soft, gentle, energy-sharing and guiding way when Cecilia is more open.

Cecilia said that Akasha has started sending her the message that Cecilia should mirror her. Cecilia describes Akasha as an amazing presence, very wise and calm; she can create everything around her into a place of peace.

Cecilia realized that the day she and her husband got Akasha, their lives immediately started changing. In their effort to address her bad behavior, they had to look inside at their own lives. As they adjusted and increasingly lived the lives they wanted, Akasha grew happier and better behaved. Cecilia changed careers, and the couple is planning to move to another country; they are on quite a different course from when they started. Cecilia said even her friends comment, "Wow, your dog really changed your life!"

Gene and Victor

Gene Leon saved his horse Victor's mother a day before she was to be sent to slaughter. Only then did he realize she was blind. Because she was unable to act like a normal mother, her foal, Victor, was not socialized normally. As he got older, Victor would charge, kick, rear, and strike at anyone he thought was entering his territory. Gene realized he needed more horsemanship skills to handle Victor, who became a strong, good-sized horse; Gene couldn't ignore the danger he posed. Some of the trainers Gene worked with questioned whether Victor was mentally stable; others thought the horse should be put down. But Gene had saved Victor and bonded to him; he couldn't bring himself to euthanize him. Gene also felt that more was going on than he understood and that there had to be some solution. Gene began to study horse training and behavior. As he learned more, he realized he had been "blind" to horse communication in Victor's early days, and he had inadvertently

Gene and Victor

contributed to much of Victor's aggression by not setting boundaries and curtailing the behavior. Gene felt that as he learned more and gained more experience, he would be able to help Victor.

This began a long journey of exploring solutions. Gene studied the methods of a number of well-known natural horse trainers and incorporated the techniques that seemed to work the best with Victor. Natural horse training techniques tend to be more humane than traditional horse training done using restraints and whipping. He also learned animal communication and began communicating honestly and openly with Victor before and during work sessions. This improved things — but only to a point.

Then an incident occurred that made Gene reevaluate his entire approach and changed his life in ways he couldn't have imagined. Victor was by then seven and a half years old. Gene was picking up the empty feed buckets one evening, and as he approached Victor, the horse swung his hind end toward Gene in a threatening way. Gene moved to correct him. Then Gene ducked through the fence as Victor backed into it, trying to kick out at Gene. Gene felt that he needed to discipline Victor, so he threw the empty feed bucket at the horse. Victor responded by whipping around and rearing, challenging Gene head-on. Gene threw a couple stones at him until Victor finally settled.

Gene was shaken up. He couldn't understand what triggered Victor's aggression, and he didn't like that he had resorted to fighting back. Things had been going well, and he thought that he and

Victor were well past this. Gene called me for help. I communicated with Victor and offered Gene a few suggestions: he should check in on his own feelings and energy before interacting with Victor and use the technique of making a mental movie of the desired interaction beforehand, explaining exactly what you want the horse to do and why. Then I asked Gene, "Do you think there might be some anger management issues here?"

Gene thought I was talking about Victor, but I was directing the question toward him. Gene said he considered himself to be a pretty calm, peace-loving person, so how could he have anger issues? Then again, he realized, he had just thrown heavy objects at Victor. Perhaps he did have some issues after all.

Over the next couple of days, little by little, Gene realized just how unhappy he was about his life at that time. He was in debt, his horse training work was not producing much income, the roofs on the farm were leaking, and he did not have the life partner he longed for. In fact, Gene felt quite overwhelmed, and he realized he

Kinna and Gene

often approached Victor carrying feelings of deep frustration and anxiety.

Then it dawned on Gene that much of Victor's unwanted behavior might be due to the tension Gene himself brought to their interactions. The possibility that Victor was mirroring Gene's own feelings of frustration made him more aware of his own energy. He started doing a "check-in" of his energy and the animals' energy before beginning an interaction, and he worked on clearing his anger and frustration before being around Victor. Gene said he noticed a definite correlation between his anxiety level and Victor's behavior. Time with Victor and other horses steadily became more harmonious and enjoyable.

Most important, Gene said, this awareness helped him to change his life for the better. He believes it is no coincidence that, as he became more and more aware of his own energy and emotions, other aspects of his life began to sort themselves out as well. Four weeks after the rearing incident with Victor, Gene met his life partner, Kinna Ohman, during one of my teleclasses. They did an exercise together on their animals and mirroring. He and Kinna now live in Vermont on their own farm, with Victor and three other horses. They plan to do horse rescue and are writing a great blog about the farm.[5] They have renamed Victor "Spirit," a name that befits their now much calmer and happier horse.

Influences to Consider Outside the Realm of Mirroring

Things are not always about mirroring. Each species has characteristic behaviors. For example, horses nip at each other to maintain the herd hierarchy. The fact that a horse will nip at a human is not necessarily mirroring, but how a person decides to deal with a nipping horse can lead to mirroring. Similarly, horses spook easily, dogs like to run off and go exploring, cats tend to fight and be territorial, and when an indoor cat gets loose, it can tend to revert to the wild, even if only temporarily. Any behavior or characteristic that reflects the genetic inheritance of the species or breed is just how things are and doesn't constitute a mirror.

Animals can also have their own spiritual agendas in life separate from their relationship with their people. Perhaps you have experienced an animal who feels like an old soul, wise and grounded, while another animal seems to have no clue what life is all about. You can see the same in people. To me, this relates to reincarnation, and the idea that some of us have been on this earth possibly many times before in other lifetimes. I, personally, feel certain that animals and people do reincarnate. My colleague Gerrie Huijts has given this issue a lot of thought over the years and believes that animals, like humans, can also have their own issues related to their soul's journey. She has come up with four categories of souls, explained below, based on the concept that animals and people reincarnate and come back in different forms to live on the earth many times. You don't have to believe in reincarnation to discover mirroring in your animals. But, for those who do believe in reincarnation, you will find the following analysis of interest. Ultimately, the issue of reincarnation is something that may only be settled when we die — that's when we will know for sure whether it is real. If you are interested to learn more about it, many good books have been written on the subject.[6]

Gerrie's four categories for types of souls are useful to help you understand what may be going on with your own animal. If you like, you can use her system as an overlay on top of the various forms of mirroring defined in this book. This soul analysis is one additional factor that may help you understand your animal and ultimately yourself.

Implicit in this model is the idea, which is popular in New Age quarters, that we, both humans and animals, decide before we come into a body what we want to do and be each time we inhabit the earth. This notion feels right to me. According to Gerrie's scheme, a soul chooses one of four basic purposes. Animals then exhibit different behaviors depending on which category they chose. I am sure as you read through the descriptions and examples, you will be able to think of some people and animals you know or have encountered who fit each category.

Category 1 — Souls Just Want to Have Fun

This category includes souls that just want to experience being a horse or cat or dog for fun. Nothing wrong will happen to them, they will have a great time — they have arranged for their life to be like this. People call this "Sunday's child," someone who always has a nice life. As with each of these categories, you will be able to observe this in animals as well as people.

Category 2 — Out-of-Body Souls

This describes souls who have no clue what they are doing, that they are souls, or that they chose to be on earth. Gerrie says she uses intuitive communication to coach animals in this category and help them remember that they are souls, that they chose to be in a body, and that they can create their reality. In this category are those who have a total lack of connection with the body. Gerrie saw this in a hospital where she once worked: people with diabetes would come in to have a foot amputated, then come back to have the leg taken off, then be back again to have the other foot amputated, when diet and lifestyle changes could have prevented this. Part of the characteristic of this group might be a complete lack of desire to figure out and address the problem. She had a serious case with a horse who would auto-mutilate and throw himself against a wall repeatedly. Gerrie had to do a lot to turn him around, including energy healing and shamanic journeying. Often if you see this behavior in an animal, some person surrounding the animal, such as the owner or a child, will behave in the same or a similar manner.

Category 3 — Life Is a Psychodrama

Most of us will fall into this category, which includes souls who, life after life, have not been able to resolve some big theme, like trust, love, love of self, being abused, connecting, letting go, being free, or forgiveness. What is nice about dealing with this situation in an animal is that often an animal communicator can talk to the animal about this, offer counseling, and possibly recommend an appropriate flower essence (see the Appendix for more on this), and the animal will be able to make a big change. It's harder for humans to just let go of these issues.

Gerrie told me the story of a horse who for many years was so stiff she could only walk. The owner had done lots of things to try to help, including bodywork, but the horse didn't improve. The horse talked to Gerrie about all her former lives, and together they determined that the issue the horse was dealing with on a soul level was trust. As it turned out, the owner had major trust issues as well and was very rigid, so horse and owner were mirroring each other. When you cannot trust, you become very rigid and defensive. Gerrie talked to the man about trust and about how this issue was reflected in his horse, and he understood. Gerrie said he took wholeheartedly to the healing process and immediately went to his horse to tell the horse that he understood about the trust issue and that he planned to go into therapy to address it. Two hours later, Gerrie got a call from the man saying that as soon as he said that to the horse, the horse galloped over to him across the pasture — something the horse had not done for years.

Category 4 — Buddha Souls

These would be the animals who act like spiritual teachers. They don't have much to resolve for themselves, but they are here to help their people and possibly other people heal, grow, and be happy. They are able to go beyond the rational mind and get people to listen and understand. When a person gives you some advice, you can just pass on it, but when you hear that same advice from your animal — either via mirroring or directly via a mediated conversation with an animal communicator — you believe it and follow the advice. Animals go straight to our hearts.

Exercise: Negative Mirroring

Are there any animals, now or in the past, who challenged you or acted out? Write about each animal and describe what happened.

Based on what you have learned in this chapter, how might that behavior have been a mirror for you?

Exercise: Special Souls

How would you describe the souls of your animals, past and present?

Make a list of your animals and after each one note down if you feel her or she was a free spirit, had real difficulty being in body, had some major issue to work through, or was a Buddha soul type, just here to help us all heal.

CHAPTER

In Sickness
and in Health

A nimals can mirror our illness, take on our physical issues, and become ill as a way of mirroring some emotional issue or as a nonverbal way to communicate some need. However, it is also always important to consider when illness and disease are caused purely by environmental factors. I encounter cases every day that could best be addressed by a liberal dose of healthy food and holistic animal care practices. I often tell people who call about a sick animal that they don't need me, they need a holistic veterinarian. While mainstream veterinary medicine is critical for certain aspects of care — like operations, teeth cleaning, diagnosis, and so on — if you want your animals to thrive on a day-to-day basis, go with healthy organic diets and holistic daily care.[1]

A good book on holistic care for dogs and cats is *The Nature of Animal Healing* by Dr. Marty Goldstein.[2] Dr. Goldstein asks, rhetorically, why so many young dogs are coming to him with cancer. The answer, reiterated throughout his book, is that conventional animal diet and care regimes recommended by mainstream veterinary medicine are not healthy. Dr. Ian Billinghurst, the Australian veterinarian who originated the bones and raw food diet for dogs and cats (a.k.a. the BARF diet), has come to a similar conclusion.[3] Commercial dog and cat food came late to Australia. Before then, people fed their pets table scraps, and ranch dogs got leftovers from slaughtered livestock. Once commercial food arrived, household companion dogs and cats started getting diseases like diabetes, arthritis, and cancer, but ranch dogs and cats remained healthy. Why was this happening? Because eating real whole food (and I will add, organic) that is close to what animals would eat in the wild keeps animals healthy; processed commercial foods do not.[4]

Health problems are not about mirroring if your animal has eaten bad food, or a vaccine makes your dog sick — except perhaps in the larger sense that human society does so many things to harm our shared environment and collective health that this situation has become a huge mirror informing us that we have to change. But if you are, in good faith, trying to take care of your animals in the best way you know how, and they become ill from some commercial pet food or other environmental threat you didn't know about, it's not your fault. I didn't always know about holistic feeding and care practices. However, now that I do, if I were to insist on feeding my dog some crummy dry food from the grocery store, then any harm this caused to my animal's health *could* be my fault. Deliberately not caring properly for my animal would represent some dysfunction in me; my animal's getting sick from this would be the negative mirroring.

Everything that applies to domestic dogs and cats applies to horses, too. Horses need to be free of chemicals and drugs as much as possible, given vaccines conservatively, fed like horses and not like cows, given good holistic care, and provided with comfortable tack (saddles and bridles).[5] A lot of horse people don't know that feeding only alfalfa (at least the type grown in the western United States) can result in kidney damage to horses and can form deadly enteroliths in a horse's intestines.[6] This information has been around a long time, but still people feed their horses straight alfalfa.

To do this knowing the threat involved would indicate some dys-function, and mirroring is at play.

When Sickness Reflects Mirroring

Once all environmental causes are accounted for, the fact remains that animals can and will get sick as a way to tell us something and help us heal and change. In fact, getting sick is clearly one of the primary ways that animals act out to tell us something is wrong.

I interviewed Dr. Goldstein about this and he told me that he consistently sees animal patients present the same or similar ail-ments as the owners or some human member of the animal's house-hold. This can even happen when the animal has a rare condition, and the owner, it turns out, has it as well. He said this tendency hap-pens so much it is uncanny, and in his opinion, it represents an ob-vious emotional connection between animals and people that can express itself in the physical mirroring of ailments. Goldstein got support for his suppositions from an obscure book he came across called *Your Pet Isn't Sick: He Just Wants You to Think So*, written by Herb Tanzer,[7] another veterinarian who recognized the emotional mirroring at work in animal diseases and disabilities.

As an example, Dr. Goldstein described a couple whose beagle had a complex heart condition. Dr. Goldstein first referred the dog to a cardiologist, who recommended a list of heart medications for the dog. When Dr. Goldstein told the clients what medications were needed, they exclaimed in surprise, since both they and their daughter were taking the same ones. The couple went on to explain that the whole situation was very odd to them: the dog had been healthy the prior year when living with the man's brother (who was healthy), but the beagle developed his heart problem after he came to live in a house full of people with heart problems.

There are some key reasons why this kind of thing can happen. Animals are extraordinarily sensitive to energy and things going on under the surface. They are now used to predict seizures in

humans and to smell out cancer. One cat at a nursing home became famous because of her ability to act in a certain characteristic manner whenever someone was getting close to death. What
this means is that animals are all-too-keenly aware of whatever is
going on inside of us, whether on a physical or emotional level. In a
domesticated situation, this is amplified, since animals find themselves inextricably placed at the center of our world, unable to leave
or take control of their own circumstances. There you have the in-
gredients for mirroring. Animals express what is going on around
them because they can't help but do this, and if they are stuck in
an untenable situation, they express the household's problems and
their concern all the more as a cry for help. Goldstein believes that
people may unconsciously select an animal who has the same or
similar problems they do — a case of choosing something in your
own likeness. When the opposite occurs and animals take on their
people's illness, he sees it as the animals' way to be in sync and
help try to heal. All the animal medical practitioners I interviewed
agreed that the healthier you are, the healthier your animal will be.
There was consensus on the converse also: when an animal starts to
get better, the person starts to get better, too.

In her practice, holistic veterinarian Dr. Lisa Pesch finds that
humans and their animals display similar problems, perhaps because, as she's observed, humans seem to have an unconscious attraction to animals with similar problems.[8] She adds, though, that
it is probably unavoidable that animals will absorb the emotions
and thoughts of those around them. Dr. Pesch has noticed that
some animals are stronger than others when it comes to dealing
with problems with their people, not unlike the differences among
humans. Some animals can handle it better and easily play the role
of caretaker, while others will cross over into taking on the symptoms or diseases of their people, a process that could be called co-
dependent.

My animal chiropractor, Dr. Maryanne Kraft, said she often

feels that an animal creates a condition that will cause the owner to bring the animal in for treatment, when in reality it is the owner who has the greater need for her services. Someone will bring in his or her dog, and within a few minutes the person will describe a physical problem he or she has. Often, Dr. Kraft noted, this is the same problem the animal has, and when she clears the issue for the owner, the animal inexplicably gets better, too. I think this happens because the animal knows it is safe now to let go of the mirroring; there is no need for it anymore.

Physical Symptoms, Emotional Causes

Frequently, what is going on in the body relates to our emotions and thoughts. There are those who say that all disease and all physical symptoms start out as negative emotional conditions, or as belief systems that then lead to negative emotions. I'm sure this is often the case, yet, as I have discussed, it isn't always true. One has to take possible environmental causation into account. Once that is done, consider the potential for an emotional component to illness, since if it exists, clearing the emotion could clear the condition, or at least aid in that process.

Louise Hay is a pioneer in this field. Her book *Heal Your Body*[9] is a comprehensive guide to her system of physical problems and the mental/emotional conditions that cause them. Here are a few physical symptoms and the corresponding causes Hay identifies:

- Fatigue — lack of love for what one does in life, boredom
- Sprains — anger and resistance, avoiding moving in a specific direction in life
- Heart problems — lack of joy, hardening the heart

What I find interesting about the approach of looking for the emotional core of a physical illness is that it brings in one more tool to use for helping an animal heal. You should pursue all the normal medical treatments, holistic care, and the like, but you can also address any possible underlying emotion at play. Then by talking intuitively with the animal, you can learn about the situation, give the animal counsel, and if need be, change things to improve the animal's life. This constitutes a truly holistic approach to animal care.

There are other systems of analysis besides Hay's. Energy healer Julie Motz[10] has written many books that discuss the role repressed anger plays in creating heart problems. The developer of the Dutch flower essence system, Bram Zaalberg, has written an excellent book about how things that happen in the body relate to what we are doing, or not doing, in our lives.

Taking on Stress

The following two stories are concrete examples of how animals can physically mirror our stress and the difficulties we have in everyday life. We just rarely take the time to observe that this is happening. For example, my student Kati Gabor described how one year when she and her partner were going through a dire financial situation, the anxiety in the home was palpable. Her cat, Tiger, ended up in the animal hospital with urinary problems. A year later this happened again when another stressful period triggered health issues for *both* her and Tiger. Then, of course, it was easier to see the connection because it happened to her at the same time.

Judith and Rixt

Judith Poelarends works part-time as an animal communicator and part-time as a researcher in dairy farming and animal welfare in the Netherlands.

She has a university degree in animal science and has had some struggles with the whole identity of being an animal communicator. Judith sees this conflict clearly expressed by her fifteen-year-old mare, Rixt. She received Rixt when the horse was one year old, as a

Judith and Rixt

gift from a friend who bred horses. Judith says Rixt is the best gift she has ever been given in her entire life. Together they have a lot of fun riding and just being out in nature. She and Rixt have much in common; for instance, they are both introverted and hesitate before joining in with others.

Recently, Judith started to notice that Rixt sometimes had skin problems on her legs, and that it was especially bad on the right hind foot and leg. Normally, horses can get skin problems when the pastures are muddy, but Rixt's problem appeared randomly, and Judith could not make any sense of it. According to Bram Zaalberg's analytical system, which Judith follows, skin problems are related to issues with the outside world, and problems with the right hind leg are about following your proper path in life, something that has been on Judith's mind for many years. Judith said that at one point the skin flare-up was really bad for Rixt at the same time that Judith was also having issues with her right hip and she was going back and forth about what to do in her life: should she keep working or start her own animal communication practice? Should she tell her friends and coworkers that she does animal communication and not worry about what they think? Was she making any progress at all? Judith was convinced that Rixt, her lifelong friend, was mirroring Judith's worry and internal conflicts.

Realizing this, she has begun changing things in her life and for Rixt. First, she told Rixt that she was aware of the mirroring, thanked the horse for showing her the issues, and told her she could let go of the issues now. Judith also followed a flower essence therapy program for herself and Rixt. Finally, she has resolved to reconcile her two careers. After Judith took those actions, Rixt's skin issues improved.

Happy Cat and Carol

This story is from Carol Gurney about how her cat helped her get in balance. At one point, Happy Cat, a gray Pixie Bob, suddenly developed a habit of constantly, almost obsessively, licking herself to the point of licking the fur right off her legs and belly. Carol tried everything: acupuncture, herbs, ointment, chiropractic work, massage, Bach flower remedies, several veterinarians, and changes in diet. But Happy Cat wouldn't stop; she just kept licking and licking. Carol was desperate to get her some relief but didn't know what more she could do. She kept asking Happy Cat what was wrong, how she could help, but Happy Cat offered no answers, either. Eventually, Carol stopped and asked herself, "If this situation happened to one of my clients,

Carol and Happy Cat

what would I do? What would I suggest to them? What usually is going on when an animal isn't able to tell me why they are doing something?" Then the thought struck her, "Could it be mirroring? Is she mirroring me?" Carol then asked herself the question, "What might I be doing constantly and obsessively?"

When Carol became an animal communicator, she started working from home, surrounded by her animals. They usually entertained themselves during the day, realizing she was engaged in her work. As Carol thought some more about this, she realized Happy Cat had begun another unusual behavior. At five o'clock most evenings, she would now jump up on Carol's desk and sit on her phone and her computer keyboard. After encouraging her gently to move away, or paying no attention to Happy Cat, Carol would continue working, and Happy Cat would continue licking. Suddenly, Carol figured it out: Happy Cat was trying to show her that she, too, was being obsessive, that she was working too hard and it was time to stop. So Carol did stop, hard as it was for her. She set a more reasonable schedule for herself, balancing work with more play time. Once she did, Happy Cat changed, too. While some of Happy Cat's issues were indeed physical — and she needed craniosacral work to subdue impulses her nerves were sending to her legs and belly — most of her licking was driven by Carol's behavior.

Taking on Symptoms

Animals can actually take on our symptoms or physical conditions, or do things that mimic those symptoms. Sometimes this is to help us cope, and sometimes it is to show us that what we are doing is out of balance.

Glen and Thunder

Glen Darlow had a lovely husky cross named Thunder whom he rescued as a puppy while teaching English and living on a Native reservation in northwestern Ontario. Glen has suffered from

Glen and Thunder

Crohn's disease since 1989, a condition that affects every part of the alimentary canal. His symptoms can include lethargy and, if he eats too much or the wrong things, severe stomach cramps and indigestion. After Thunder died from cancer in October 2011, Glen noticed that his pains had gone away. Glen wondered if Thunder was somehow sending a message that he was still there, looking out for Glen, and perhaps even taking the pain away from him. As time passed, he felt sure of this. He even tested it by eating freshly baked bread late at night, which would normally cause horrendous cramps. But he had no pains. This reprieve lasted for months, then eventually his symptoms returned. But it didn't matter to Glen, as he felt sure of what his beloved dog had done for him.

Marie-José and Lady

Marie-José Hakens, who took my workshops in the Netherlands, is a psychologist and another expert whom I consulted for this book.

She completely understands the concept of mirroring and says she deals with it daily with her clients. From her point of view, everything in your life and in life in general is a mirror (which I discuss further in the Conclusion). With her expertise and experience, Marie-José was able to see rather quickly when her dog, Lady, began to mirror her.

Lady is a charming and lovable Cavalier King Charles spaniel. Cavaliers are very sweet dogs who have a fatal genetic flaw related to the size of the skull, which causes them to have epileptic fits. This is a largely manageable issue, and a holistic approach helps, but it is often unavoidable in the breed. Marie-José, however, began to notice that Lady's fits were, to use Marie-José's phrase, "mirror-messages" for Marie-José herself on several occasions.

Lady's fits correlated with her own state of mind whenever she would go into mental "overload." When she would find herself completely in her head and almost buzzing with the electricity of her thoughts, she would see a corresponding reaction in Lady, who would have an epileptic fit. Marie-José described her mental state as kind of drowning in stress and worry, the opposite of a peaceful state of mind. Once she recognized that Lady's epileptic fits were mirroring her own state of being, she thanked Lady for the information and immediately took some holistic remedies to mentally calm down. The first time she did this, Lady's fit almost immediately subsided. The mirror aspect was clear, and Marie-José became determined, for Lady's

Marie-José and Lady

sake, to remain more aware of and responsible for the state of her own energy.

The Message in the Mirror

Animals can do more than just mirror our stress or our bad back with their own physical health. An animal's illness can sometimes be a deliberate message for us, an attempt to wake us up to our own unproductive behaviors or poor life choices. By getting sick, an animal can try to save us from ourselves.

Beth and PornStar

Beth Riedel is a landscape gardener and an animal nutritionist and herbalist. Even though she worked daily with sick animals and the emotional conditions surrounding illness, it took her a while to see what her cat was doing for her. Beth says that he changed her life well before she ever knew about the ability to communicate intuitively with him.

Beth and PornStar

It all started when Beth took in a stray orange cat she named Cornbread, whose name soon seemed too tame for the cat's personality. He was a very self-assured male who went after what he wanted until he got it, though he was very sweet and loving to those he cared for. He literally forced his way into Beth's home whenever the door was open. A neighbor dubbed him PornStar, and the nickname took. Beth said that whenever her on-and-off relationship with a particular man was going poorly, PornStar would get an abscess in his groin. The cat would get better when Beth stopped seeing the man. But she was basically "addicted" to this particular man, and she kept reconnecting with him despite her own ambivalence, and PornStar kept getting abscesses.

One day, as she was teaching a class and telling the students how she had observed pets in families with terrible communication skills getting frequent bouts of ear mites, and suddenly she "got" what was going on with PornStar. She felt so bad for her dear cat. She took care of his abscess, never dated the man again, and got counseling to deal with her emotional issues. PornStar lived another eight years and never had another incident.

Pauline and Leila

Pauline Ticheler consulted Gerrie Huijts about her cat, Leila, who was diagnosed with a bone tumor on the left side of her jaw. The veterinarian took an X-ray, told Pauline that Leila had cancer, and recommended a very expensive surgery followed by chemotherapy as the only option. The fur on Leila's cheeks started falling out.

Pauline and Leila

When Gerrie interviewed Leila intuitively, the cat insisted that nothing was wrong with her, and she kept repeating to Gerrie the numbers three and four. Gerrie told me that when an animal does that she now knows that it means something important happened in the person's life at that age. In particular, if you ask an animal his or her age and get a wrong number, that is a clue to look into what was happening with the person at the age the animal relayed. Gerrie pressed Pauline about the numbers, and it prompted Pauline to recall that when she was four her three-year-old sister died of a bone cancer in her head. For some reason, it appeared that Leila wanted this to be discussed. Gerrie and Pauline explored the issue of the sister's death at length. Meanwhile, Leila insisted that she would be fine and everything was fine.

A little while later, Pauline took Leila back to the veterinarian to get another X-ray to check up on the tumor. After the second X-ray, the veterinarian could find no evidence of a tumor. Leila's fur grew back, and today, as she claimed, she is just fine.

Showing Us a New Way

The next two stories illustrate how an animal's behavior can change our beliefs or show us a completely new perspective on life — one we probably could not have gotten any other way but through our animals.

Tallanny and Carol

Tallanny was Carol Gurney's first horse, a handsome Arabian gelding. When he was twenty, Tallanny became seriously ill: he developed a severe case of hives that resisted all treatment. Then his body became covered with six-inch sacks that oozed serum, and eventually his legs developed ulcers that bled constantly. Carol sought the help of a number of veterinarians, but none of them could help her horse. Next she turned to every other approach she knew: herbs, acupuncture, holistic care, but still, nothing worked. Tallanny handled it like a trooper, but Carol agonized over him and her inability to make things better. As she says, "This one brought me to my knees. I felt helpless. I just couldn't do anything for him to make it stop. I felt totally out of control."

From the moment she met him, Tallanny and Carol shared a

Carol and Tallanny

special connection. She met him at a training ranch and began to take lessons on him. She felt drawn to him, and to her delight, when he became available for lease, she jumped at the chance to make her connection and commitment to him more official. After her lessons she would just hang out with him in his corral, grooming him, cleaning the bridle and saddle, or just sitting with him in total silence. Carol was a Type A, on-the-go ex-New Yorker, so it was hard for her to be relaxed and quiet, but around him, she felt different. She felt like all her problems just went away, and she felt more loving, peaceful, relaxed — as if she had all the time in the world. Meeting him changed her life, and Tallanny became her best friend, the one who gave her the courage to believe in and trust her dream to listen to animals heart to heart. He was the one with the quiet strength, spirit, and wisdom who showed Carol how to begin her own journey of personal growth and how to live a heart-centered life. And now the one who had helped her the most was the one she was unable to help.

Carol was angry: the veterinarians had no answers. She was also sad, scared, depressed, and felt inadequate. If she didn't do something soon, she was going to lose her horse. The emotions Carol experienced as she watched Tallanny struggle were almost unbearable, and they kept growing stronger until all she felt was sheer, raw pain. It was as if every pain she had ever experienced in her life was coming back to her. All those things she had buried reappeared, just the same as Tallanny's wounds, on the surface, and she realized she finally had to deal with them.

Carol says this began a whole new part of her life. Now she understood what Tallanny was trying to show her, and she was able to tell him: "Tallanny, I get it, I understand. Now please let me handle this, you need to let it go." Carol began a personal quest to discover the source of her pain, which she addressed in various therapeutic ways. The moment she made the commitment to address the issues Tallanny had shown her, Carol discovered a veterinarian who had the answer: a medication that dealt with Tallanny's rare autoimmune condition.

Today, Tallanny is still with Carol. As of the writing of this book, he is thirty-eight years old and continues to help her and teach her important life lessons.

Annemieke and Cevesta

Annemieke Kleen has a twenty-eight-year-old mare named Cevesta who came into her life fifteen years ago when the mare was thirteen. Cevesta remains in very good condition, and the two go riding together three or four times a week. One day she was riding Cevesta just after her cat Inci had died unexpectedly at a young age. Annemieke was grieving about the cat's death. At the end of the ride, Cevesta, whom Annemieke recognizes as a mirror, began to go lame. The next day the horse couldn't walk at all and was in severe pain. Cevesta has a history of laminitis, an inflammation of the feet, and it was clearly flaring up again, but Annemieke suspected that the lameness might also be related to the grief Annemieke was feeling over her cat Inci.

She consulted a veterinarian who was also an animal communicator, and they had an extensive talk with Cevesta about her lameness. Cevesta had much to say to Annemieke about her grief and about how to manage grief and still keep functioning. At the

Annemieke and Cevesta

end of the session, Annemieke felt somehow that this time she would not need to do all the medicines and treatments she would normally have to use for laminitis. She also felt that Cevesta would recover very quickly. That is exactly the way it turned out. Because Annemieke was open to the messages from her horse, Cevesta got better in just two weeks rather than two months, and they were off riding again.

Annemieke says she is deeply touched by the love of this wise and lovely horse. The veterinarian told her that the reason Cevesta is so young and healthy at twenty-eight is because she is being heard and seen.

Life on the Line

On some occasions I am convinced that animals are just flat out trying to save their people. One story that I will never forget, which

I tell in my book *Beyond Words*, is about a woman who was an alcoholic. When she stopped drinking, she went to the doctor for a checkup. The doctor told her that he couldn't believe she had ever been a drinker because her liver was fine. Shortly thereafter, her cat, who used to lie sprawled across her stomach at night, died of liver cancer. The following two stories are other examples of animals working to save their human companions.

Renee and La Bamba

One day in her home in the Netherlands, Renee Nieuwendijk Hoek was watching her herd of horses and knew something was wrong with her son's young mare, La Bamba. The mare was lying down, and even though another horse was pushing at her, she would not stand up. As she watched, a sudden storm came up with lightning, thunder, and heavy rain. Renee went inside thinking that the storm would make the mare stand up, but when she returned fifteen minutes later, the herd had moved to the other side of the field and

Renee and La Bamba

La Bamba was still lying down. Renee rushed over to her, phoning the veterinarian at the same time. She screamed and yelled at the mare, kicking and pulling to make her stand up, shouting, "Don't you dare leave me!"

Renee somehow managed to get La Bamba on her feet and to the stable, but once there the mare lay down again. Renee was exhausted and could not get the horse up, so while waiting for the veterinarian to come, she sat beside La Bamba, pulling the mare's head onto her lap, and crying and talking to her. Renee told La Bamba that Renee's son would be home soon and would spend more time with her. She told La Bamba that he had big plans for her and the mare needed to keep on living.

Then Renee heard La Bamba distinctly say, "And what about you?"

She knew instantly what La Bamba meant. At the time Renee was in a severe depression. She had lost everything she owned and was trying to find something to live for again.

She knew that La Bamba was saying, "What's it going to be? Will we do this together?"

She knew that La Bamba needed Renee to get back on her own feet again, too. As Renee held La Bamba, she opened up to her totally, telling her how much she loved her and that they would always be together. Then Renee stood up, straightened her back, and told La Bamba, "Now it is your turn: get up, now!" She said the horse stood up, passed some gas, shook herself, and looked at Renee with the softest gaze she has ever seen.

The veterinarian came but could find nothing wrong. He took blood samples, but again, found nothing. Renee says that La Bamba gave her a reason for living again and is her most precious animal. La Bamba is doing fine now, and so is Renee.

Linda and Joe

I met Linda Allen at a workshop in Vermont. She told me this story about a horse named Joe, whom she bought when he was three and

Linda and Joe

she had just turned fourteen. A Thoroughbred–quarter horse cross, Joe came from somewhere out West. Skinny and gangly, he'd probably had a saddle on him once or twice but had little more training than that. Linda had taken riding lessons for two years, had a tiny budget, and her parents knew nothing about horses. Joe was handsome and the price was right — so he came to live in their barn. Right from the start, she and Joe had a tumultuous time. He bucked, crow-hopped, and bolted. He tossed her hundreds of times. He spun and reared while being led from the barn to the paddock. On several occasions, Linda watched helplessly as he jumped his own paddock fence and ran off to the next field to graze.

She didn't have the money to pay for lessons, so she had to figure out Joe's training on her own. Somehow over the next few years, she says, they forged an understanding, and he learned that galloping across a field with a person on his back could be fun. They even began to do a little showing, and although he got to be pretty good working in an arena, he was happiest galloping in the open and cross-country jumping. At one point she discovered that she loved him, and she is pretty sure that he loved her.

When Joe was six years old, Linda had to sell him in order to go to college, and he went to live with a doting owner who began eventing with him, a discipline that includes dressage, cross-country jumping courses, and show jumping, which evidently he took to immediately. But then Joe died at age nine. Joe's death was neither his owner's fault nor Linda's fault, but for decades afterward Linda felt horribly guilty about Joe. For nearly forty years, she was haunted by a recurring dream in which she suddenly realizes that she has forgotten to feed Joe or take care of him, and in her dream she runs to the barn to find him in his stall. When she gets there, he says, "Where have you been? You forgot to take care of me!" Linda always believed this dream expressed her guilt at being unable to save Joe. She said she was often able to sense Joe's presence, as if his head were hanging over her shoulder.

In the workshop in Vermont, we did a visualization to meet a spirit guide. Linda thought that Joe might show up as her guide, and sure enough he did. But nothing really happened. In the journey, she and Joe stood there for a while and then walked around in the woods. She didn't feel that much, and Joe didn't reveal anything. A bit frustrated, just as she was preparing to leave the journey, she asked Joe why he had come. He answered, "Because I am you." And with that, Linda understood that in all those dreams he had been trying to tell Linda to take care of herself. Before Linda ended the journey, Joe agreed that Linda could call on him for assistance anytime. There would be no more restless dreams; now they would be partners.

Helping Us on Our Path

It is clear to me from these final stories that the animals involved were leading their humans down the intuitive path. That is the path of your heart, the path from which your inner voice speaks. It can be really hard to follow that path. It means you have to pay attention to what you truly need, not everyone else's needs. You have to listen to your own counsel even when it is contrary to what everyone else is telling you. This is one of the hardest things to do in life. Is it any surprise that our animals are right there helping us learn how?

Georgina and Janssen

Georgina Buitendijk's dog Janssen, a Rhodesian ridgeback, became ill, was unable to hold down any food, and stopped eating. Georgina contacted a holistic veterinarian, who told her that there were problems with his liver and his kidneys and gave her holistic remedies to use. The medicines didn't work, so Georgina went back to the veterinarian. The veterinarian had been trained in animal communication and also in mirroring issues. She evaluated the situation from that perspective and told Georgina she sensed that some problem Georgina was having with a person was also affecting Janssen. As soon as she said this, Georgina started crying, realizing what Janssen

Georgina and Janssen

was trying to show her. She was having serious issues with her roommate at the time. During the months that Georgina lived with that person, she was losing her strength, giving away her power, and falling into a negative, destructive pattern from her childhood. That was what Janssen was showing her. He lost his strength also, and he could hardly walk.

After this realization, she went for a walk with Janssen, although he didn't want to go. She stopped in a meadow and had a serious talk, telling him that she knew what he was showing her, and promising him that she would solve the problem and get her strength back. She also told him that she was very worried about his not eating. She asked him if he would please start eating. She told him again his job was done, the message was understood. Janssen started eating the next day. A few days later Georgina had an argument with the roommate, and the roommate decided to leave.

Georgina says she has learned to look at her dog and to ask herself, "What is he showing me today?"

Grace and Henri

Grace Thutyakul has two older horses, and she has asked me to help with them in the past. Then one day I got a call from her that I was dreading. Grace said that her older horse, Henri, was unable to stand, and the veterinarian was recommending she put him down. Henri was diagnosed by the veterinarian as having spinal damage from arthritis.

Grace asked me to talk to Henri and find out what he wanted to do. When I tuned in to Henri, he said he was in a lot of pain, but he didn't want to die. He also told me that he felt he could get better.

Henri did ask me if he could be moved to be with his friend, Grace's other horse, who was recently moved to another barn. Henri was being boarded in a retirement home. He told me that he really did not want to be there without his friend. When I checked in with Henri, I didn't get the feeling he had spinal damage. I advised Grace

Grace and Henri

to get a horse bodyworker to do a session with Henri and see what transpired. Through our combined efforts, we found someone to come see Henri on an emergency basis. The bodyworker did some craniosacral work, and Henri responded well, but he was still very wobbly and had a hard time getting up and staying up. Nor could he walk any distance without circling.

People continued to urge Grace to put Henri down, and the bodyworker soon joined in the refrain. Grace and I and Henri were the only ones going, "Hmmm, no, let's wait and try something else." I kept getting from Henri that his feet hurt, so Grace went and got him some horse tennis shoes. This seemed to help a bit but not enough.

At the darkest moment, Grace told me that she sat in the paddock with Henri's head on her lap. When she saw his eyes rolling back and only the whites showing, she said to him, "Okay Henri, I guess I will just have to let you go. I don't want you to suffer, and everyone is saying I should put you down." As soon as she got out her cell phone to call the veterinarian, Henri's head came off her lap and he looked at her. Then, she said, he got up and mustered all his will to walk over to the water trough and take a drink. At that point Grace told Henri, "Okay, I guess you will be the one to tell me when to call the vet, and I guess that would not be anytime soon."

Grace arranged to move him back to the stable near her home where her other horse resided. People were so skeptical and disapproving of her actions that she had trouble finding someone to help her trailer him. But the miracle was, he slowly started to improve. A few days after the move, he had improved to the point where he could walk without falling down. After that he steadily got better. Grace found out that the actual cause of his problem was a well-meaning but inexpert hoof trimmer who took too much off Henri's soles and toes. All that time Henri had been suffering severe foot pain, not spinal damage from arthritis. Henri is now completely recovered and a very happy boy.

Through this experience Grace learned what it feels like to follow your own truth in spite of intense counterpressure from those around you. This is a life lesson she will never forget, and she has Henri to thank for it.

Exercise: In Sickness and in Health

Choose an animal who is in your life currently or an animal from the past, and consider any illnesses, major injuries, or incapacity of any kind that the animal is experiencing, or experienced in the past in his or her lifetime. Based on what you have read so far about mirroring, do you see any patterns or any possible mirroring between you and your animal that could be going on now or could have happened in the past with regard to any of these conditions?

Look in the Mirror —
What Do You See?

When someone contacts me to do an intuitive session for an animal, if I start to get a feeling that there could be mirroring going on, I go into what I call "ponder mode." I find myself just sitting there and thinking about what mirroring could be going on between the person and the animal. When I do this, I usually have my eyes closed. I might find myself cocking my head first one way, then the other. I will "think up" toward the top of my head, the way Pete Sanders recommends in his book *You Are Psychic!*,[1] and I will ask the "Universal Library" — which is what I call all the knowledge in the universe — for information on what kind of mirroring could be happening.

Slowly, bits of information will start coming through to me. I might get a feeling that the person is really worried about another person, and then get the word *partner* and the impression of people arguing. Then I might see an image of the animal being equally worried and frantic; at that point, I might suspect that the animal could be taking on the person's worry. The person who called may have seemed completely relaxed when we talked on the phone. They may have described their issue as being about a dog who barked too much, or some other typical animal behavior problem. But when I get back to the person and ask if there could be some stress with a partner or spouse, usually I will find that I have hit the nail on the head. That's how I get at the issue of mirroring for other people, and it's a completely intuitive process. However, when I set out to see mirroring between myself and my own animals, it's a different story.

It's hard to see your own issues, and it's hard to see your issues mirrored in the behavior of your animals. To help you do this, I have designed a questionnaire and other diagnostic tools, which I present in this chapter.

Before you complete the questionnaire, here is a short review of how mirroring works. There are four categories or modes of mirroring, which can overlap:

- Emotional
- Mental
- Spiritual
- Physical

The mirroring dynamic can be:

- Positive, negative, or neutral
- Direct or indirect

The following questionnaire covers all these areas and should help you identify how your animals may be reflecting your feelings, thoughts, beliefs, or physical conditions. Some of the questions may seem repetitive, but they are asking for similar information in a slightly different way, to help you capture as much detail as possible about your animal. As you complete your responses, you may recognize that your animal is expressing some unresolved, perhaps long-standing issue you have. This is mirroring you may want to address.

Use a separate notebook to answer the questions in the questionnaire, or copy these pages first; this way you can complete the questionnaire for as many animals as you want. You can choose to work with a current animal or one from the past. If you want to see trends between your animals, complete the questionnaire for additional animals and compare the results.

Once you complete the questionnaire, I explain how to compile your answers into a case study report. At that point, you can start "cleaning the mirror" using the techniques I present in chapter 7.

My Animal, My Self
Mirroring Questionnaire

Animal Name _____

SECTION I: HOW YOU GOT TOGETHER

1. Write down everything you can remember about how you found out about your animal. Include when, where, and how you met.

2. What made you focus on that specific animal?

3. What attracted you to the animal?

4. Why did you decide to purchase, adopt, or rescue that animal?

5. Can you identify any themes between the adoption of this animal and the adoption of other animals in your life?

Go back over your answers above and circle anything in what you have written that you think might represent a mirror, positive or negative, between you and your animal. For example, that you felt sorry for the animal because he was lonely, and you felt lonely at the time you found him.

Section II: Positive Qualities

1. List all the positive things you can think of about this animal.

2. What do you particularly love about this animal?

3. What are the strengths and good qualities of this animal?

4. What do you admire about this animal?

5. What skills does this animal have?

6. How is this animal special and unique?

7. What good things have people said about this animal?

8. What is lovable, attractive, and cute about this animal?

9. What good things has this animal done or caused to happen?

10. What are the positive qualities of this animal?

Go back over your answers above and circle anything on your list that is a match in some way for you. Put a double circle around anything about your animal that you would like to either adopt or intensify in your life.

Section III: Negative Qualities

Some of the questions below may not apply to your animal, in which case you can answer N/A (not applicable).

1. List all the negative qualities you can think of about this animal.

2. What don't you like or what particularly bothers you about this animal?

3. What are this animal's weaknesses, vulnerabilities, or bad qualities?

4. What does this animal do poorly?

5. What do you find unattractive about this animal?

6. What negative things have people have said about this animal?

7. What is *not* lovable, attractive, and cute about this animal?

8. What bad things has this animal done or caused to happen?

Go back over your answers above and circle everything on your list that is a match in some way for you or that could be a situation where your animal is trying to show or tell you something about yourself.

Section IV: Physical Qualities

Record whatever you know about this animal's physical condition, past and present. If the animal is a rescue, you may not be able to answer every question fully.

1. What diseases or illnesses has this animal had in his or her lifetime?

2. List all other symptoms, pains, and medical conditions this animal has or has had.

3. What major accidents, injuries, physical trauma, and incapacities has this animal experienced in his or her lifetime?

Go back over your answers above and circle any conditions you listed that also apply to you now or in the past. Also circle anything that you think may be a mirroring situation between you and your animal.

Section V: In-Depth Questions

1. What about your animal is challenging for you?

2. How does your animal act toward you? What might that indicate about your core beliefs about yourself?

3.   Have you ever experienced a relationship before that is like the relationship you have with your animal? If so, when, where, and with whom?

4.   How does your animal make you feel? When have you felt that way before, and in what context?

5.   Who do you know or have you known who is like your animal?

6.   What situation does your experience with this animal bring to mind? Record all the details you can remember about that previous situation.

7.   Are there ways you act that are similar to the way your animal acts? What are they, and are they things you don't like?

8.   What do you think and feel when your animal does something you don't like? Have you felt that way before? When and in what context?

9.   In what ways might you be contributing to your animal's negative behaviors or condition?

10. What do other people say about you and your animal? Have you ever heard the same things said in the past in relation to you or your life?

11. What do you think and feel when your animal does something good? Have you felt this way before in your life?

12. Is there something you don't like about your animal that you also dislike and want to change in yourself?

13. If your animal is acting in a negative way, how might this be mirroring for you?

14. How is what your animal does a reflection of how you feel about life?

15. What is your animal's behavior, emotion, or physical condition leading or requiring you to do in response? How might this be a mirror for you?

16. Is there some way that your animal's behavior, emotion, trauma, or physical issue is making you look at something buried in yourself?

17. If the animal has died, what were the circumstances of the animal's death, and do these circumstances mirror any other traumatic event in your life?

18. If the animal has died, how did you respond emotionally to the animal's death, and does this reaction reflect any pattern you have?

Go back over your answers above and circle any responses, whether ongoing now or related to the past, that you think apply to you and that may be a mirroring situation between you and your animal.

Section VI: Identify the Most Significant Answers

You should have a lot of circled answers in Sections I through V of the questionnaire. Each answer you circled could be a mirror between you and your animal. Usually, people are amazed at how many characteristics they share with their animals. Now go back over your answers to fine-tune your results.

Go through each section and evaluate your circled answers. Are many of them related or seem to be about the same issue, or are they extremely varied? Based on the instructions below, use a highlighter or put a star notation next to those answers that you determine are most significant.

Section I: How You Got Together

Highlight or star anything in this section that is an issue you are struggling with, or anything that you are striving to incorporate into your life. Your animal represents that for you. Also identify any recurring themes in terms of the animals you adopt.

Section II: Positive Qualities

Highlight or star any positive qualities your animal is showing you that you would like to have but don't feel you do, or don't feel you have enough of.

Section III: Negative Qualities

Highlight or star any negative qualities that were a match for you and your animal that you feel you would like to address by lessening or getting rid of them in both of you.

Section IV: Physical Qualities

Physical ailments can suggest underlying emotional issues with your animal. To help determine this, consult the "Physical Symptoms Chart" below, on page 144. For each answer you circled in the "Physical Qualities" section above, see if you can find the corresponding condition on the chart. If so, note the possible underlying significance the chart indicates for this physical condition, and write in whatever further information the chart provides about you and your animal.

For example, if you circled ankle problems as a common physical ailment for both you and your animal, consult the chart for the possible related core emotions, thoughts, or traumas associated with ankle problems. The chart indicates this can mean several things: you may have a problem with how strong you are in life, or you may not be well grounded, or you may be inflexible. If any of those is a match for you and your animal, record that additional insight.

Once you have annotated your answers for this section, go through and highlight or star any answers that are a strong match or any physical conditions that you think your animal is exhibiting in order to show you something about yourself. Also highlight any physical conditions your animal has that you want to resolve, regardless of whether there is a match or a mirror with you. For example, the mare I recently adopted has a limp, which is unrelated to me or any mirroring situation. I will, however, include the insights in the charts and the techniques in chapter 7 as part of my overall approach for resolving her physical issue.

Section V: In-Depth Questions

This section is more qualitative, and it reveals the dynamics of your relationship. You will need to interpret your answers to identify what specifically is being mirrored. For instance, negative reactions that you have toward your animal may reflect negative judgments you have about yourself. Answering the in-depth questions should have given you a good idea of what the important mirroring issues are between you and your animal.

Highlight or star any answers that indicate mirroring going on with you and your animal that you feel you want to lessen or get rid of.

Physical Symptoms Chart

The following chart identifies some common ailments in humans and animals and the associated emotions, beliefs, or traumas that could underlie those conditions. I collected this information and compiled this chart using a wide variety of sources, primary among them the work of Louise Hay, Bram Zaalberg, and Dr. Ryke

Geerd Hamer.[2] Note that this is not a comprehensive list of diseases and conditions; moreover, all the sources I used reference human disease, not animals, so their information is not expressly designed for use with animals. See the Notes section at the end of the book for my main sources and helpful links. However, if you and/or your animal has one of these conditions, take a look at this chart of possible underlying causes and see if the information resonates with you. Could your animal be holding a symptom or condition so that you will take a look at the associated emotion, belief system, or trauma? If this doesn't resonate with you, trust that reaction or understanding and move on. The information in this chart is meant to help you gain insight about you and your animal, not put you in a box.

Zaalberg has done an extensive exploration of what he calls the emotional regions of the body, and I provide here only a brief summary of his work. He identifies the right brain and the left side of the body as feminine, associated with feelings and intuition. The left brain and right side of the body is masculine, associated with thinking and acting in the world. Whatever occurs in the back side of the body pertains to something in the past; alternatively, issues on the front side focus on the future. So, for example, an injury to the right shoulder would indicate a problem going forward in life as well as a potential issue from the past that may be holding you back. Look over the physical issues and ailments you listed in Section IV above, and pay attention to which zone of the body is affected to correctly identify what mirroring might be involved.

Dr. Hamer is an expert on cancer, and according to his research, the real cause of cancer and other diseases is the experience of unexpected traumatic emotional shock. His treatment for cancer includes therapeutic sessions to identify and defuse the traumatic experience. Only a small portion of his information on target organs in cancer and the associated conflict emotions is incorporated into the chart.

Condition/ Location of Problem	Possible Related Core Emotions/ Thoughts/Trauma
Abscess	Pent-up thoughts over hurts, slights, revenge
Accidents	Rebelliousness, inability to stand up for oneself
Arthritis *(also assess the affected region of the body)*	Self-criticism, resentment of others, inflexible thinking, lack of forgiveness, difficulty asking for help
Allergies *(also see "skin issues")*	Denying own power, aversion to someone
Ankle problems	Problem with how strong one is in life, being inflexible, being ungrounded
Anxiety	Not trusting life to support one's efforts, fear
Asthma	Feeling stifled, suppressed
Autoimmune diseases	Conflict with self, guilt, self-hatred

Condition/ Location of Problem	Possible Related Core Emotions/ Thoughts/Trauma
BACK PROBLEMS: *Lower*	Fear of lack of material support, denigrating self
Middle	Guilt
Upper	Feeling unloved, lack of emotional support
BLOOD PROBLEMS	Lack of joy, stagnation of ideas and life
BOWEL ISSUES *(including constipation)*	Fear of letting go, holding on to past
BREATHING PROBLEMS	Not feeling one has the right to exist, fear of taking in life fully
CANCER: *General*	Hurt, resentment, secret grief, futility
Bladder	Ugly conflict, dirty trick
Bone	Lack of self-worth
Brain	Stubbornness, refusal to change, mental frustration

Condition/ Location of Problem	Possible Related Core Emotions/ Thoughts/Trauma
CANCER *(continued)* *Intestines*	Anger
Kidney	Not wanting to live
Liver	Fear of starvation
Lungs	Fear of dying or suffocation, fear for someone else
Pancreas	Anger, conflict within family
Spleen	Shock of physical or emotional wounding
Stomach	Excessive anger
Thyroid	Feeling one lacks power
Tumor (any location)	Nursing old hurts and shocks, building remorse
COLIC	Mental irritation, impatience
DIABETES	Longing for past, need to control, being overly sorry, no sweetness

Condition/ Location of Problem	Possible Related Core Emotions/ Thoughts/Trauma
Diarrhea	Fear, rejection, running off
Ear problems	Inability to listen to others and/or to oneself, anger or too much turmoil
Eye problems	Problems with perspective on outside world and self, fear of present or future, inability to see joy, not wanting to see what is happening
Glaucoma	Being unforgiving, pressure from past hurts, feeling overwhelmed
Foot problems	Lack of connection with earth, emotional strength, or understanding of self and others, fear of future, not stepping forward in life
Gastritis	Prolonged uncertainty, feeling of doom
Heart problems	Lack of joy, dealing with life from anger, long-standing emotional problems, not taking time for oneself, not listening to oneself, insecurity, perfectionism
Hip problems	Fear of going forward in life, feeling one has no perspective on life

Condition/ Location of Problem	Possible Related Core Emotions/ Thoughts/Trauma
HYPERACTIVITY	Fear, resistance to change
IRRITABLE BOWEL SYNDROME	Anxiety, feeling like a victim, unwillingness to change
INFLAMMATION	Anger, seeing red
JAW PROBLEMS	Anger, resentment, desire for revenge, inability to deal with the emotions of others
KIDNEY PROBLEMS	Criticism, disappointment, failure, shame, unresolved grief
KNEE PROBLEMS	Being inflexible, too much pride and ego, uncertainty about own feelings, uncertain connection with outside world
LEG PROBLEMS	Inability to go forward in life, fear of future
LIVER PROBLEMS	Anger and rage, chronically finding fault in self and/or others, chronic complaining
LUNG PROBLEMS	Inability to embrace life, depression, grief, feeling unworthy to live

Condition/ Location of Problem	Possible Related Core Emotions/ Thoughts/Trauma
Mouth problems	Closed-mindedness, not feeling nurtured
Nausea	Undigested ideas and negative emotions
Neck problems	Stubbornness, inflexibility
Pancreas problems	Anger, rejection, disillusionment with life
Parasites	Giving power away to others
PMS	Internal conflict about being female, unwillingness to go with flow of nature
Skin issues	Overly sensitive, out of touch with self or others, fear, anxiety
Seizures	Running away from family, self, and/ or life
Shoulder problems	Difficulty carrying experiences, considering life a burden
Sores	Unexpressed anger that settles in
Spleen problems	Being obsessed about things

Condition/ Location of Problem	Possible Related Core Emotions/ Thoughts/Trauma
STOMACH PROBLEMS	Dread, fear of the new, not feeling nourished
TOOTH PROBLEMS	Indecisiveness, an inability to approach things logically, taking life too seriously, lack of acceptance, anger
THROAT PROBLEMS	An inability to speak up for oneself, swallowed anger, stifled creativity, refusal to change
THYROID PROBLEMS, GENERAL	An inability to express oneself emotionally
Hyperthyroid	Selfishness, fear of responsibility
Hypothyroid	Feeling repressed, hopeless
ULCERS	Inflexibility, fear, stress, anxiety, unresolved issues, lack of self-esteem
URINARY TRACT INFECTIONS	Blaming others, anger
VOMITING	Violent reaction to ideas, fear of the new
YEAST INFECTION	Denying one's own needs, not supporting oneself

Section VII: Make a Case Study Report
for You and Your Animal

Everything that you have highlighted or put a star next to represents a mirroring situation between you and your animal that you want to address. To clarify and distinguish this from any other issues, it is helpful to make a case study report. I have provided a template below, and afterward I have provided a completed report, so you can see what it should look like. The case study report I did was for my white quarter horse Sophie.

To compile your case study report, simply copy the items you highlighted or starred in the questionnaire into the case study report form below.

Case Study Report

Animal Name _____

How I Got This Animal/What I Was Drawn To

Positive Qualities

Positive Qualities This Animal Is Modeling for Me

Negative Qualities

Physical Conditions (and Interpretation from Charts)

In-Depth Questions

Sample Case Study Report: Sophie

Below are the results of my own case study report for Sophie, the white mare whom I described briefly in chapter 1. Here is a little further background on Sophie. I got this mare from a friend from whom I also adopted Mojave, my mustang. Mojave and Sophie are in love. I didn't want to take him away from her, and my friend didn't want Sophie. Sophie was severely abused to the point of sadism by a previous owner. If you say one harsh word around her, she will simply take off to the hills. She was terrorized and has not recovered well from it. She was also allowed to stand with a broken bottle shoved up into her front foot for we don't know how long. As a result she is lame. When I first got her, I couldn't catch her. She is terrified of people. Now we are pretty good. I can catch her, pat her, work on her feet, and kiss her; we are friends. But if anyone else shows up, she's off to the hills. I have given her about five names so far. Sometimes, I do this with the animals I adopt; I

Mojave and Sophie

will just go through names until I find the one that fits. Right now, I think Sophie will stick. I was looking for a name that was soft and sweet and a counterbalance to all she has been through, a name she could grow into and that expresses the animal I hope she can become.

I did this analysis with her to help me figure out what is what with her. While her behavior has improved since I got her, I still want to shift what is going on for her even more. In chapter 7, I continue this analysis of the mirroring I have found between Sophie and myself by presenting my plan for how to address it. Not everything below is negative; my plan of action for Sophie will include strategies for eliminating negative mirroring but it will also include plans for enhancing the positive.

For some of the items that were a match, I added an explanatory comment. A match doesn't mean complete mirroring; it could be that just a small part of you resonates with a corresponding quality in your animal.

How I Got This Animal/What I Was Drawn To

She was isolated, depressed, and alone — I feel this way at times.
Really sad — I can be, too.
She had no options — Sometimes I feel that way.
She is white — I like white horses, but then I like black, brown, and red horses, too...LOL!
No one wanted her — I can feel that way sometimes.
She was a challenge — I like challenges.

Positive Qualities

Healthy
Pretty
Soft eyes
Very sweet

Positive Quality She Is Modeling for Me

Her connection with her life partner. This is something that attracted me to Sophie and something that I aspire to.

Negative Qualities

Nice to a fault — I can be
Super sensitive — True for me
Bit bossy to other horses, can be hard to deal with — I can get bossy
Scared of men — I can be too sometimes, but not like she is.

Physical Conditions

Abused, mistreated — I have had some of that in my life, but nothing like what she went through.

Serious leg injury, front left, and she has problems with her right hind leg — I had a serious injury to my right hip from a fall and couldn't move well for a few years. According to Zaalberg's analysis, the right side in back has to do with going forward in life and being held back by issues of the past. She and I both have that as a mirror.

In-Depth Questions

She makes me see I need to walk my talk more and do the work on her. She needs bodywork, and I need to do Carolyn Resnick's waterhole ritual work[3] with her. This work is done without ropes or halters, in an open area, and the horse is free to choose whether to leave or to connect with you. Through a series of activities, you show your horse that you can be trusted and that you are the leader, but a kind and fair leader. Sophie is also forcing me to find ways to get all my other animals to comply with my requests without raising my voice, since that makes her take off. She is showing me I have too much anger.

Sophie is starting to feel a little like my inner self, and I am thinking I may need to get some extra help, just like Sophie needs.

CHAPTER 7

Cleaning the Mirror

There are many ways to make change happen in your life. I will tell you some of the techniques I like and show you how to use them. Often, the best technique for you will be the one that feels right — that's your intuition at work. Try my suggestions and be open to other new healing modalities that you may encounter.

Decide What You Want to Fix

Go over your case study reports. From the highlighted items (or from the trends you identified), pick one issue you would like to focus on. If you are like me, you will be saying, "I want to do them all, not just one." I understand, but for the purposes of testing out the techniques presented here, pick one issue and work through the various sections of this chapter focusing only on that issue. Once you are familiar with the techniques, then you can start tackling multiple issues, or all of them, and work through them simultaneously. I am always working on changing more than one thing at a time; that can be done, but it's easier if you start with just one issue.

Fix Things Physically

If you discover that you and your animal are mirroring the same physical condition, take actions immediately to resolve your own problem. Then look for ways to physically help your animal with the problem. Check out my website for holistic care resources for dogs, cats, and horses. Then, of course, there are many alternative modalities to choose from for healing the body, including energy healing, bodywork, flower essences, essential oils, and so on. The list is endless. For example, if you have a bad back, get yourself treated by a really good bodyworker — someone who does muscle release work or a chiropractor — and then do the same for your animal. Once the immediate physical symptoms are addressed, you can work on healing any emotional component that might be behind the physical problem, first in yourself and then in your animal. You may find that when you address a mutual problem in yourself first, it immediately resolves in your animal.

In the case of my horse Sophie, who is a tough nut to crack, I will probably end up doing just about everything I mention in this chapter. I want to fix her fear and also cure her lameness. To help with the latter, I plan on finding a good flower essence formula for her and also some herbs, and I will do bodywork on her and train her using the Carolyn Resnick method.

Fix Things Emotionally

The advice is the same for an emotional problem as for a physical one: fix the issue in yourself first. For an emotional issue, that may mean getting counseling, doing energy healing, or changing an aspect of your life so it no longer plagues you. Getting some bodywork is never a bad idea; it can help you to relax, stop worrying, and be more in the moment. Once you begin this process with yourself, you can then look at helping your animal with the emotional issue (often in many of the same ways). See also "Use Some Aids" below.

Resolving an issue that is recurring and deep-seated can be tougher. It will definitely be helpful to get counseling or work with a life coach for support. Louise Hay talks about this in her book *You Can Heal Your Life*.[1] Her take on repeated negative patterns is that there must be some need in you to create this pattern. She says to start simply with the willingness to release the need for this pattern in your life. She suggests using the affirmation, "I am willing to release the need for [whatever pattern you want to release]." In the section on manifesting below, I give instructions for working with affirmations to make them as powerful as possible. I have found affirmations to be a very effective way to change beliefs and make your life more positive.

Spirit Talk

Sometimes the reason for mirroring is some conflict or problem that can't be resolved through direct interaction. The spirit talk technique is used for talking to people or animals whom, for whatever reasons, you can't or prefer not to talk to directly. For example, in the case of an animal, I use this technique to help animals connect on a spiritual level with the people who abused them. I advise my human clients who are having a problem with a person, or even with an animal, to use this technique to connect with that individual without having to actually confront them in reality. This process is very much like intuitive communication. Even though you are using your imagination, it is real, and whoever you are addressing will actually hear what you say.

To start out, imagine meeting the person or animal you want to address in some imaginary place in nature. Make this place as real as you can. If you feel you need protection for this meeting, imagine bringing along anyone you like who could fill that role. Then, imagine talking to the person or animal and saying everything you would like or have been afraid to say. Perhaps these are things you simply would not say in real life, or you would not expect to be heard if you did. Listen and respond to what the other individual has to say until you feel the conversation has come to a close. Then thank the individual and end the talk. This technique can change minds and shift the energy of a situation in amazing ways.

Use Some Aids

When I say "use some aids," I mean use physical adjuncts like crystals or essential oils, both of which can aid in healing. Flower essences are also an excellent choice for shifting things to the positive. You can use them for healing your body, your emotions, and for improving anything negative that is going on in your life. For more on Dutch flower essences, which is the system I particularly like, see the Appendix.

Talk with Your Animal

Talking with your animal about negative mirroring is one of the most effective tools you can use; it's easy and you can get instant results. When I teach people how to communicate intuitively with animals, I tell them, "Talking is the easy part. "In my previous books, I discuss how this type of connection with animals and nature was common in indigenous cultures, but it has been lost in our modern world. It's an ability that everyone has, even if we don't realize we have it. To communicate intuitively with an animal, all you need to do is talk to your animal out loud as if you are talking with a person. When you talk out loud, it is the same as sending your thoughts mentally. You can also think what you want to say and your animal will pick it up. Talk out loud and in depth about the negative mirroring issue with your animal. In addition, it is important to tell your animal four things:

1. Tell your animal you understand that he or she is mirroring you to help you.
2. Express thanks and appreciation for how much your animal cares about you.
3. Confirm that you really want to resolve the issue and are committed to doing so.
4. Explain that you would like your animal to let go of the issue now and release it. Tell your animal that you can't grow and move on until the issue is released by both of you. Ask your animal instead to become a positive mirror for you and lead the way toward both of you becoming happier and healthier.

For complete instructions on how to receive information intuitively, read one of my previous books. But in short: after you talk to your animal, note and record any intuitive impressions that come to you. These impressions could be feelings, thoughts, or images. Your job is to perceive and record these impressions without trying to analyze them — after you have them recorded you can sort through and evaluate them. If you can keep your critical mind disengaged and just record what comes in, you should, over time, get proficient at getting your animal's messages. If you find, however, that no impressions come to you, then you have to jump-start your intuition. You do that by forcing yourself to make up a response. This primes the pump of your intuition, and you will find that impressions start coming spontaneously.

Use the Coach Approach

Treat your animal as though you are a coach and your animal is an Olympic hopeful. This means you believe your animals can change, and you communicate to them that you are doing everything you can to support that change. This is the approach you should take when working to clear unwanted negative mirroring.

Metaphysical Techniques: Manifesting

This category of techniques involves using your intention — your thoughts, visualizations, and emotions — to create change. Energy healing, which I recommend that you explore for both physical and emotional issues, is also a metaphysical process. There are many different energy healing techniques; explore the ones that sound good to you and let your intuition help you decide which ones to pursue.

Manifesting means combining thought and emotion into an intention that will affect the quality of the energy around you, as well as the energy surrounding a present or future event. There are a lot of books on how to manifest for change,[2] and I have been studying this topic for many years. I include here the techniques that have worked the best for me.

Affirmations

To make affirmations as powerful as possible, say them often. Write the affirmation on a sticky note and put it on your mirror. Then say this affirmation to yourself whenever you look in the mirror. It may seem a bit odd, but I have found that writing the affirmation, putting it on the mirror, and then saying it out loud makes it come true.

Make your affirmation short and powerful. It should be a phrase that really expresses your dream and makes you happy when you say it. For example, with Sophie, I plan to do bodywork with her to help her heal and do groundwork training to help her see me as a trusted leader. My affirmation for this could be, "Sophie loves me now and she is totally sound."

In addition to posting your phrase and saying it often, you can also share it with your animal. Describe your affirmation as the dream you have for what can happen. So I would say to Sophie, "Sophie, my dream is for us to be best buddies and for you to be sound and riding the trails."

Making a Movie

At least once a week, and as often as once a day, spend a minute or two making a movie in your mind of what you want to achieve. Imagine this with all your senses. Focus especially on how you would feel and what you would think if your dream for yourself and your animal were to come true.

You can do this with your animal as well. First, tell your animal out loud what your dream is, and then make a movie in your mind to show your animal what you mean. For Sophie, I would close my eyes (but only close your eyes around a horse if the horse won't then decide to stomp or bite you) and imagine her coming to me with trust, moving without a limp, and us riding together on the trail.

Your animal will understand your words and see the movie as you play it in your mind — it will be like a template you are providing for the future.

Making a Vision Board

A vision board is a visual cue to your subconscious for what you want to manifest. I have one in my office that I see whenever I look up from typing. I cut out pictures from magazines that express what I am working to achieve and put key words up that catch my eye, like "What I visualize, I materialize." Make a vision board for yourself concerning the negative mirroring you want to shift. Place the board so that you can see it regularly. This will help shift the energy to the positive.

Being Grateful

Take time every day to be grateful for whatever good has happened in the day or the recent past. You could be glad that you feel healthy, or grateful for the vegetables growing in your garden; anything large or small that comes to mind is appropriate. Make sure to acknowledge any good changes that happen. Don't treat them as coincidences. Realize that changes are happening because of your intentions. The more grateful you are, the more you will experience positive change coming into your life.

Taking on Your Animal's Positive Mirror

In the chapter 6 questionnaire, you may have identifed something positive about your animal that you would like to accept as true about yourself as well. Form it into a short sentence. For example, if you found that you and your animal are both fun-loving, but you feel that you would like to bring more fun into your life, make that desire a short, simple declarative sentence, perhaps something like: "I have more fun in my life." As with any affirmation, the phrase should be short and presented as if it's already happening. Then post this on your mirror and say it to yourself daily. This will help you incorporate this quality more into your conscious experience.

Changing Negative Beliefs

Do you believe you can change? If deep within you don't believe change is possible, you won't be able to change. How we feel secretly inside, and the thoughts we project unconsciously, affect the experience we have in life — thus the axiom: what you think about, you bring about. If it is hard for you to believe change is possible, you may need to look at what beliefs underlie your negative feelings. Do you believe things have to be difficult, or that you aren't competent enough to take good care of your animals? Brainstorm to find any hidden negative beliefs you may have, related to your animals. Then use the techniques below to change negative beliefs into positive beliefs. The way Louise Hay describes it,[3] you have to have faith that the Universe wants you to succeed and will support you. Using these techniques, you can align your thoughts, emotions, and actions in a positive direction so you can enjoy your animal from the perspective of positive mirroring and eliminate any negative mirroring that you may have discovered.

If you find that you have a negative belief that is holding you back, determine the core of that belief. For example, if you believe your animal can't heal from an injury, the core of that may be that you feel you are not competent for the job.

To derive the core of a negative belief, ask yourself what beliefs lie behind the thought or feeling.

Now decide what beliefs you would prefer to have instead. Per the example, you would change the negative belief to something like: "I am great at helping my animals heal."

To instill your new positive belief, pay attention whenever the old one comes up in your mind, and when it does, say or think, "Cancel that belief." Then say or think the new belief. It will also help to post the new belief on your mirror and say it out loud to yourself daily. I go over this technique again in the book's Conclusion, where I discuss how to change negative beliefs that may be holding you back in your life.

Metaphysical Counseling for Yourself

One of the more helpful and interesting things I have done for myself in metaphysical counseling is to get someone to do what is called a past-life regression session. The counselor uses hypnosis to help you recall your past lives. I was particularly interested in past lives when I might have done animal communication. In the session, I recalled a few of my lifetimes, and in one of those lives I was killed for doing this work. I realized that some of my hesitation about telling people about being an animal communicator came from that lifetime. Once I had the past-life session, and realized that my fear was not relevant to this lifetime, it was much easier for me to talk about my work.

Counseling Your Animal

It helps to talk things over with your animals and give them your best advice on how to change any negative mirroring situation that you discovered. You can also help your animals change any negative beliefs they have, and work with them on any past-life issues they may have, as described below.

Helping Your Animal Change Beliefs

Animals often have an easier time than we do of changing negative beliefs. Sometimes if you just talk with them and explain that there is no need for the belief and that it is harmful, they will simply let it go. Explain out loud or mentally to your animal the steps for identifying and clearing negative beliefs. Then encourage them to go through this process on their own.

Animals have the ability to manifest, too. Explain the techniques for manifesting to them out loud or mentally, and encourage them to start manifesting.

Working with Past Lives and Your Animal

If you already know how to do animal communication, you can ask your animal to tell you about any past lives that may still be creating problems in this life. My experience is that animals are much more aware and remember a lot more about past lives than people do. If you don't know how to communicate intuitively with your animal, you can ask a professional to help you with this. Often if there is some past-life issue, you will have a feeling that this may be the case — that's your intuition at work. Not all animals have past-life issues that need to be resolved, but if you have tried to solve a problem in every other way and still don't have a solution, this would be one more thing to try.

Also review the soul analysis that was presented in chapter 4 (see pages 100–103) to see which soul category fits your animal. Is your animal a soul that just wants to have fun, an out-of-body soul, a soul trying to resolve a psychodrama, or a Buddha soul? Then explain the situation to the animal and help him or her understand what is happening in this life, if the animal needs this kind of help.

Working with Your Guides

A guide is any being, living or in spirit only, who wishes to help you in any way. Who could be your guide?

- A living animal — one of your own or any domestic or wild animal
- The spirit of any animal
- A current friend, relative, partner, or teacher
- The spirit of any person
- Any aspect of nature, living or in spirit
- Any spirit being who comes forward who wants to help

I believe you can have multiple guides; I do and it seems to work well for me. I have different guides for different purposes, too — some for healing, finding lost animals, and so on. I ask for help from my guides in the moment whenever I need it. I believe they are waiting for us to ask for help so they can step in, and I ask for a lot of help! Another technique is to ask your guides for help when you awaken and right before sleep. Ask them to show you guidance, intervene to help, and lead you in the right direction. You can focus these requests on resolving the negative mirroring you want to clear.

Take five minutes during the day to sit and brainstorm about how to clear your negative mirroring. Your guides will come through with information at those sessions, and you will find that information just starts popping into your head throughout the day, so be prepared to record those flashes of insight; have a notebook at the ready or else, as has happened to me, you might have the thought and then forget it. Make sure to record everything even if it doesn't make sense or seems impossible; later on you may find the wisdom in what you have written.

Spirit guides like to hear how helpful they have been. Make it a habit to do this daily. I like to do it while I am driving. If you have a major cause for celebration, make sure to thank your guides for their part in the event.

Shamanic Journeying

Most indigenous cultures have a tradition of shamanic journeying.[4] Journeying means traveling in spirit to connect with those in the spirit world and to ask for guidance and help. This is another technique that can help solve negative mirroring situations. When you take a shamanic journey, your body stays in the present but your spirit travels, as in a dream, although you are not asleep. Often a shaman or someone trained in that tradition will facilitate your journey using drumming and other practices, but you do not need a guide to journey to the spirit world. You can do it on your own.

To conduct a shamanic journey on your own, record yourself reading out loud the script I provide below. As you read the script, drum softly, like the heartbeat of the earth in the background. At the end of the script, use a different, faster drumbeat as a signal to come back to your body. There are an infinite number of journeys you could take. For example, you can journey to meet a power animal, your totem animal, an ally in nature, a healing ally, and so on. This journey is to get counsel for a negative mirroring problem.

Journey to the Council of All Beings

On this journey you will travel to the Council of All Beings to seek their advice. Before you begin, set your intention to find the best way to address the negative mirroring you are working to clear between you and your animal.

Close your eyes and imagine yourself in whatever setting you like, a place in nature that you love. Now look for your messenger guide who will take you to the council. Once you meet up with your messenger, you can ask his or her name and ask if the guide has a message for you. Follow your messenger guide to the council meeting place. By tradition in shamanism, the spirits of animals and nature reside in the underworld. This is a place like our reality, the middle world, but the province of the spirits of the animals and nature. To travel there you may fly, go in a boat, go through a rabbit hole or down a tree trunk, dive into the water, or go by some other means.

Once in the underworld, go to the council, which meets down by the sea in a huge cave. After you find them, thank your messenger and go in. Who is sitting on your council? Greet them and thank them. Tell the Council what you want help with. Describe your mirroring problem.

How does the Council respond? They may give you advice, or they may want you to take a journey to see something you need to know, or they may do a healing on you, or anything else to help you with your issue. Follow where they lead.

[At this point, drum for a number of minutes without speaking, for as long as you think you will want to be journeying. It can be five to ten minutes or longer. Then start reading the script again.]

Now it is time to return. Go back to the Council meeting place, thank the Council. Go to the seashore and find your messenger. Follow the messenger back to your place in nature, and then journey back into your body.

Case Study: Rewards of Working with Mirroring

Dr. Gisela Kenda told me this story about her dog Basil, and it is an example of how our animals guide us by mirroring issues for us. It also illustrates the good that comes when we pay attention and follow the path our animals show us.

Gisela, Hanny, and Basil

Gisela got Basil when he was two years old. He had been returned to the breeder by his first owner because he was attacking
and biting other dogs and was also aggressive to people. Gisela took
the time to work with him, slowly exposing him to people and other
dogs in controlled situations and giving him lots of praise and support for being calm. Through this process, she was able to get him
to completely shift. Now he can walk through a group of children
or a group of other dogs without incident. Gisela educated him herself, and he became a search-and-rescue dog. She said that today
he likes people, though he doesn't like to be touched unless it's by
someone he knows. He goes with her off-leash and even walks right
by aggressive dogs, ignoring them totally. Gisela said he taught her
that you have to look below the surface; he is a lovely dog now, but
he started out being completely rejected by society. He also showed
her that there is nothing to fear, and finally that nothing can be
achieved with pressure.

Basil jumping in the lake

Basil climbing back on board

He went even further as her teacher. Basil was competing in rescue at a high level, and then he had an accident that made it impossible to compete anymore. This for Gisela was a mirror that Basil held up. She realized how much she had invested in the whole idea of competition. Basil had other ideas. She says he showed her that even though he was an extremely talented dog he didn't have any need to go to competitions anymore. He taught her that everyone is excellent, and there is no need to compete. Now she and Basil have fun in all kinds of sport activities, swimming or jumping from the boat — Basil taught himself to climb back up a ladder onto the boat. In winter they go skiing, and he pulls her on her cross-country skis at speeds up to thirty kilometers an hour. She and Basil are having a lot more fun now because all the pressure is gone.

Exercise: Inner Animal/Inner Human Visualization

This is a very simple meditation to use with your animal to correct any imbalances and any negative aspects that you would like to see changed. This exercise is based on the work of Bram Zaalberg. This technique is a way to adjust your internal reality (or mirror) with your animal so that it matches your dream.

First, form a mental picture, a visualization of you and your animal. This internal picture may not match the way you think of you and your animal; that's okay, just study it.

1. Evaluate your size relative to each other. Are you equal in size?

    Whoever is bigger is dominating; a little bigger is okay, but too big will be too dominant.

    Whoever is smaller will be submissive; too small is too dependent.

    Adjust your visualization to correct for these factors. Visualize yourself and your animal as about the same size, with yourself being just a bit bigger.

2. How do you each look? Are you unhappy or sick? Is anything not optimal? Correct your visualization so that you and your animal appear exactly the way you want to be.

3. Who is more the boss, you or your animal? Correct your visualization so that you are slightly more in charge, but be in balance, so your animal is happy with that.

4. Do you and your animal notice each other equally and give each other equal attention? If not, correct your visualization for that.

5. Do you each have enough personal space? If not, correct for that.

6. Are both of you facing in the direction of the future, side by side, or are you both looking back toward the past? Correct for this. Imagine both of you side by side and facing the future.

7. Look for anything else that you might want to change, like any mistrust, fear, worry, hyperness, not being grounded, or any negative mirroring, and correct for that.

8. Now interact with your animal in your visualization. How do you play? Correct for anything that is not your ideal.

9. Have you and your animal face each other and let love flow from each of your hearts to the other.

10. Put both of you in a white balloon of light and let the image go.

11. Do this once a day until you see a shift, then do it once or twice a month thereafter.

Take note of the issues and qualities that you adjusted in this visualization exercise. Consult the Appendix to select some flower essences that address these issues or qualities. Use these essences for yourself and your animal daily for at least a month.

CONCLUSION

Mirror, Mirror, Everywhere

Writing this book was instructive for me. I hadn't really sat down and systematically looked at the issue of mirroring between animals and people, much less the idea that mirroring goes on all the time between people, between people and the events of their lives, and ultimately between all beings and the earth. Doing this research has been a liberating experience for me, especially in terms of seeing everything in life as a mirror. I learned some useful techniques for analyzing and understanding the things that go wrong in your life and the traumas you experience, and I will share them with you here.

People and Life

The working assumption behind the idea that everything you experience in life is a mirror is this:

People will treat you exactly the way you feel about yourself.

Your relationships with people and what happens to you in life are showing you how you feel about yourself and what you believe. In other words, they are a mirror for you. To change what you experience, you have to accept this premise and be willing to explore it.

You will have to be careful not to feel guilty, stupid, responsible, or like a failure. It's far too easy to fall into a sort of paralyzing despair if we think we did something bad or did something to make our life bad. This process is not about judging yourself; it is about you discovering what is keeping you from being truly happy.

To find out which feelings and beliefs are not serving you in life, you can do the following analysis.

Figuring Out the *Real* Problem

I tried this out for an incident in my past when an acquaintance said something rude to me. I asked myself what I did to contribute to that incident happening. Two things came up. One is that I knew the acquaintance was not someone I really wanted to have in my life, but I was being nice and trying to get along with the person anyway. Second, I realized that this tendency in me to "be nice" stemmed from my experience growing up with two older sisters who never wanted to include me in their activities. We are all friends now, but as a child I spent a lot of time trying to get them to like me to no avail. It seems I was repeating a childhood pattern. I find I am using this new awareness to curtail associations that aren't helpful for me rather than trying to appease when it is not necessary or useful.

Questions to Ask Yourself

Here are the questions to ask yourself about any event or person that is bothering you or has bothered you in your life. Again, these questions seem to implicate you as the responsible party in what has happened, and that can feel uncomfortable. Put up with the discomfort in order to see what lies behind it. You just may have an insight like I did that will make you a lot happier going forward.

1. Identify some way you have been treated that you dislike, in the past or present. What does this indicate about how you feel and what you believe about yourself?
2. Identify something that someone else does that you don't like. In what way are you also doing that, even if only to a small extent?
3. Choose some quality about someone that you don't like. Ask yourself where that quality might reside within you, even if only minimally.
4. Identify something that happened to you that you did not like. Now ask yourself what beliefs you must have had for that to have happened. What within you let that event happen?

You can use the above analysis to defuse any situation that arises in your life. Try it with some incidents and people from the past, and you will see what a great tool it is. Through this analysis, your enemies can be converted into your greatest teachers.

Working with Your Negative Beliefs

If you do this analysis, over time you may identify some negative beliefs that you will wish to change. The process below can help you eliminate these negative beliefs and adopt positive ones. If you aren't sure what negative beliefs you have that you may want to change, follow the instructions below for how to determine that.

Process for Reversing Negative Beliefs

You can discover what your negative beliefs are by identifying the negative patterns in your life and then determining the negative beliefs that fuel those patterns. Here are two examples of negative patterns:

- You experience constant debt.
- People disregard your opinion and talk over you.

Next, ask yourself what beliefs might lie behind these patterns. For example, your beliefs could be that:

- Making money is always hard.
- You are not charismatic.

Once you have found the negative beliefs that resonate for you and appear to be operating, unconsciously, in your life, revise those negative beliefs into positive ones that you would rather have. Per the example, the beliefs could be changed to:

- Money comes easily to me all the time.
- People are interested in and attracted to me.

To instill your new positive beliefs, pay attention when the old ones come up in your consciousness. Then say or think, "Cancel that belief," and say or think the positive belief instead. It will also help to write the positive belief on paper, put it on your mirror, and say it out loud to yourself daily.

Another technique for changing negative beliefs is to act as if what you want to believe is already true, like a dress rehearsal. It can also be helpful to select past events that were traumatic and reimagine them instead to have occurred the way you would have liked. This helps to release the negative energy associated with those past events.

At the end of this chapter, I include a visualization exercise

Bram Zaalberg gave me to share with you. It will help you balance your energy and create more harmony in your life.

The World

The idea that our individual animals are mirrors for us can be expanded to apply to groups of animals, and finally to all the animals in the world. Thus we can see that the entire group of sick domesticated animals act as a mirror for all humans showing us that the conventional care methods we employ are making them ill. The toxicity of the environment is having an adverse effect on our animals. Collectively, they are showing us that what we are doing is unhealthy and bad for them. In response, more and more people are feeding real food diets to their animals and using holistic care practices. The mirror is working; it's waking people up.

Our domesticated animals are further showing us that violent training techniques do not work well. Collectively, they are a mirror for humans showing us that violence is not the way. In response, more and more people have been exploring nonviolent training techniques. The incredible amount of violence being done by humans to both domestic and wild animals is a mirror for humanity of how emotionally and psychologically ill we are becoming.

All the sick wild animals in the world and all the dying species are a mirror for how out of sync we are with the earth and with nature. Likewise, so are the traumatized and failing habitats and ecosystems — all showing us that what we are doing is bad for all life on the planet.

Author and researcher Richard Louv in his book *Last Child in the Woods*[1] identifies a syndrome in children he calls nature deficit disorder. He sees a growing problem with children raised in cities who never have contact with nature, and he attributes a variety of ailments, including attention deficit disorder, to this trend.

Everything in nature is a mirror for humans. There is a field of psychology called ecopsychology that took a leap into popular culture and didn't quite catch on. It's getting a new revival now and not a moment too soon. The basic tenet of ecopsychology is that there is no separation between humans and nature; we cannot extricate ourselves from nature. We are to the earth as a baby is to its mother. And when the mother is ill, the baby knows. In our case, we are desperately trying to ignore that fact that the earth is in a dire situation, but we know it every moment of every day, and it affects us deeply.

With so much at risk, so much being destroyed, it is no wonder so many people have gone into denial as a defense mechanism rather than holding the truth of our time in their consciousness.

The problem is, you can't run away. The fact that things are getting worse is inescapable. You can either go into serious denial, and even use drugs or some other crutch to escape, or stay conscious. Those who stay conscious are responding by going organic and pursuing sustainable agriculture and other sustainable practices. Millions of nonprofit efforts are helping turn things around on the earth, and many people around the world are protesting what is happening.

The first step toward restoring harmony is to look at what's in the mirror using the tools acquired in this book. In her book *Living in the Light*, Shakti Gawain advises us to look inside and find what we don't like in the world as it is mirrored in us. For example, if you don't like violence, find and fix all the ways you are violent, in thought and action. Perhaps you are too critical of yourself and are often angry at yourself. She suggests that you start to heal the world by healing the mirror for the world that you find within.

It is also critical to take action to change what is happening in the world as well. Seeing violence in the world, for example, the violence that is done daily to animals on such a grand scale, and doing nothing to stop it is a mirror for feeling helpless. The only way to turn that around is to start doing something and, by your actions, lessen the suffering. Then you will begin to build a mirror of yourself as powerful and this world as full of people who are powerful and compassionate. I believe that is the true reality of our world, and I do believe, against all odds and all indications to the contrary, that we will find the way to heal ourselves and our world.

Our environment reflects our inner self, though we think of these two things as completely independent. As I have discussed, the ordinary daily outer relationships in our lives are reflections (or mirror images) of our inner relationship within ourselves. The visualization exercise in the following section will help you come into better alignment with all aspects of your life. It is the template I used for the Inner Animal exercise in chapter 7, and it was written by Bram Zaalberg, who sent it to me to include for you in this book.

Exercise: Inner Woman/Inner Man Visualization

Imagine your feminine energy as if it is a woman. Try to see what she looks like: is she cheerful or glum, happy or sad; is she looking in front of her, behind her, or sideways; is she standing firmly on the ground; can you see her feet and legs, her hands and arms; is she tall or small, busy or quiet? Now make this image the most beautiful or ideal person you can imagine. While doing this, it is important that the woman looks straight ahead and is standing on your left side, which is the feminine side of your body. Now do the same with the inner male energy and imagine your inner man: what does he look like; is he happy or sad; is he lazy or active; can you see his feet and legs, his hands and arms, is he small or tall; in which direction is he looking? Make the man the most beautiful person you have ever seen and put him at your right side looking straight ahead.

Compare the man and the woman. Who is taller? The taller one will be the leader, and the smaller one has to listen to this part of your consciousness. When your woman is taller, she will be in charge, and your man has to listen. In this case, your feelings are the most important part of your being, and the thinking part has to listen to them. Adjust your mental image to create a woman and a man who have the same height, by lowering or raising one or the other; adjust the images until you are comfortable with them.

Be aware that you have to do this on a regular basis. When you use specific flower essences for the female and male inner being, this will help the process. In the beginning, a lot of emotions can come to the surface. Sometimes these are problems or emotions you thought you had already resolved a long time ago. Accept them, but don't examine them; just look at them and let them pass by. You can write down your emotions as part of getting rid of them.

Once you have corrected the images, bring the inner man and inner woman together; let them embrace and hug each other. Imagine putting a circle of light around them and let them blend over into each other. Then let this bubble of energy float away or dissipate and don't think about it anymore.

APPENDIX

Dutch Flower Essence Remedies

Flower essence remedies are one of the best ways to address any kind of problem you are experiencing. There are many different kinds of flower essence remedies from all over the world. I have included the descriptions of the Dutch Flower Essence Remedies in this Appendix because I feel they are very powerful, and I hope you will find ways to incorporate them into your life. Choose the single essence or the combination that best addresses the issues you might be working on with your animal or in your life.

Flower essences are made by placing a flower in water for a period of time, sometimes in the sunshine, and then removing the flower. The water takes on the essence of the flower and is preserved in alcohol or other preservatives and bottled.

You can read through the descriptions of the essences that follow to find one (or more) that particularly addresses any negative mirroring you identified for you or your animal. Then order the essence and use it as described to see what shifts occur. In this list you will also see some essences made for specific applications, such as relieving stress or building the immune system, and you may like to use them as well to see what results you get.

Here are some things that Bram Zaalberg, the creator of Dutch Flower Essence Remedies, says about flower essences:[1]

When you take flower essences, they help you to connect with your Higher Self. Every flower essence is a universal law or energy, a blueprint of a particular energy contained in the flower that is captured in water.

As soon as we start working with flower essences, we are starting to change ourselves; this results in a change of the outer world. Changing yourself is changing the world.

Here are some recommendations from Bram for using essences to work with your inner man and inner woman (see the exercise in the Conclusion, page 179):

Essences for strengthening the inner woman: red poppy, borage, evening primrose, Love
Essences for strengthening the inner man: orchid, little inky cap, sensitive weed, Protection, Rainbow
Essences for grounding a tall inner woman: yellow star tulip, mycena, red henbit, Terra
Essences for grounding a tall inner man: Terra, purple flower, giant stropharia
Essences for integrating male/female: greater celandine, Love, yellow star tulip, field scabious

Individual Dutch Flower Essence Remedies

The following remedies are made and distributed by Bram Zaalberg through his website (www.bloesem-remedies.com), and he provided the following descriptions for this book.

Single Essences

ALTERNANTHERA (*Alternanthera dentata*): This essence helps you to find balance in your feelings and not be afraid to express them;

to not let yourself be disturbed by other people or other issues but to keep your own counsel; to do the work you believe in and bring your Higher Truth into reality, to work with it and to expand it; to not think timidly but to give full expression to what is; to love the earth and the deepest core of your own being in the deepest way.

ANGELICA (*Angelica archangelica*): Provides protection from the spiritual worlds and the help of loving forces from on high; provides "angelic protection," especially when one crosses the threshold to the "other side," as in situations such as death, dreams, meditation, or birth. Favors a more spiritual development of the consciousness and strengthens the ability to experience loving spiritual forces in your life and work. Encourages growth, protects the consciousness, and increases trust in the leadership of the Higher Self (a "Godly" trust with a good earthbound feeling) when you are confronted with unknown areas, while freeing you from doubt about your personal wisdom.

BORAGE (*Borago officinalis*): Borage strengthens the heart in difficult circumstances and brings gladness and joy. It encourages persevering courageously, not letting yourself be blocked by difficulties, and not losing heart despite adversity. When you lose faith, borage brings back joyfulness and strength to the heart and helps you handle things with the heart rather than the head. Borage has proved effective for those trying to get pregnant, helping them to connect with the soul of the child.

CALIFORNIA POPPY (*Eschscholzia Californica*): The California poppy essence helps you trust in your feelings and listen to your heart. California poppy is calming; it gives the insight that you no longer need to look to the outside world to find what is important, but you can find it in your inner world. It brings the restfulness and peace of inner knowing. Encourages not looking for the superficial gold of fame and glory but digging deep for the gold of inner wisdom. It gives you new insights and helps you integrate these new insights into your heart. It helps you to let go of worries associated with the outer world, establishing a balance with the importance of the inner. It also brings a balance between light and darkness, fostering a spirituality of the energy of Mother Earth. Good for people who are too busy with the outside world, like those with ADHD.

CLEMATIS (*Clematis vitalba*): Clematis not only is for awakening but gives a clearer picture of your actions. Clarifying the thought processes, it improves your capacity for thought and helps you to obtain a more conscious insight into the handling of your affairs. Gives more insight, an overview of the cause-and-effect process, and more clarity to the unconscious. Used for working in and for the Light and manifesting this Light in the world around you.

COPRINUS AURICOMUS (*Coprinus auricomus*): Helps with handling things from the strong source of your original being; returning to your own structure; persevering in spite of blockages and the feeling that you cannot go further; opening your heart and getting you moving toward your future; strengthening your feminine qualities; moving on; and being open to your future. Gives strength and space to the physical body. Makes room for the new and transformation.

EVENING PRIMROSE (*Oenothera lamarckiana*): This plant flowers at night. While the red poppy brings the power of the sun into the feminine qualities, the evening primrose essence strengthens the creative forces of the moon. It helps you to (re)discover and connect with the source of self-confidence and the inner worth of the feminine. It brings insight into old patterns of incest, rape, and sexual problems, giving support and help for discussing such problems and bringing everything out into the open. Also good to use when you are dominated by a boss or an elder; it supports men and women by reinforcing their self-confidence.

FIELD SCABIOUS (*Knautia arvensis*): Grounds and supports, especially when you have the feeling of not belonging. Quiets the thinking and purifies unnecessary thoughts through the earth. Encourages positive thinking. Helps you to handle things better, to be more perceptive and open to others and the environment. Connects you to the higher, serene spheres and enables you to reflect them back out and into the surroundings so you can receive the support and warmth of others. Very good for purifying the aura. Putting two drops of the remedy in the palms of your hands and holding them within the aura purifies it and dispels even the most ancient and tenacious memories.

FOXGLOVE (*Digitalis purpurea*): Foxglove eases the mental processes so you are able to contact your heart. Helps you to let go of thinking structures and patterns of how you think you should behave, especially concerning old beliefs. Helps you to modify behavioral patterns and to be more playful in life. Gives joy and pleasure to sexuality and life in general. Foxglove opens you, step by step, to higher realms beyond thinking, so you are able to use other sources of information, such as dreams. Often these problems or difficulties have their roots in the heart or the emotional world.

GIANT STROPHARIA (*Stropharia rugosoannulata*): This essence gives new insight into the things you are doing. Instead of fixing your eyes on the difficulties in life and the things you do, giant stropharia helps you to direct your attention to pleasure and fun. It helps you take direct action, especially when you have been sitting around far too long, thinking about what to do. Encourages handling things from the heart and doing things for the fun of it and not because you feel you must or feel that it is expected of you.

Giant stropharia connects you to the earth, releasing back into the ground energies and tensions that are stuck behind your eyes.

GOLDENROD (*Solidago officinalis*): The key words of goldenrod are *individuality* and *the other*, especially in a group, when you feel locked up and cannot open yourself to others; when you are unable to let go of your personal ego and cannot direct your attention to the higher qualities; when you put your interest too much in your personal achievements; and when you feel overdependent on others. Goldenrod gives you self-trust and self-confidence, allowing you to open your being with love toward your environment, so your being can give itself with enthusiasm, a sense of abundance, and cooperation.

GREATER CELANDINE (*Chelidonium majus*): This essence is for men and women alike. It balances the right and left hemispheres of the brain, the masculine and feminine; and purifies and grounds excessive emotionality. Improves relationships, especially when a wall has gone up between people. Helps through thought and reflection to purify your feeling life, with the result that the purity of your being becomes the basis of your existence. Eliminates emotional poisons; helps you release anything that you no longer need. Instills acceptance of your innermost self, removing feelings of inferiority.

GROUND ELDER (*Aegopodium podagraria*): When you seem unable to develop further, ground elder helps by manifesting your growth, enabling you to make a better connection with your true self. When you are overoccupied with self-development, ground elder helps you to let go and opens you to the higher qualities of your being so that you no longer need to fight all the time with your environment. Ground elder is helpful when you have difficulty assimilating everything you meet; it facilitates integration and cooperation with the environment through the expression of the heart, coming from the Higher Self.

GROUND IVY (*Glechoma hederacea*): Ground ivy clears away old emotions you didn't understand. Makes you aware of and able to transform behavior patterns. For abundance, strength, and expansion, it helps with personal development and attunement, bringing out the finer qualities of your being. Facilitates trusting in your own being, wherever you might be, and helps with healing work. It is good to keep a bottle beside you, and when you meet with a painful or emotional disturbance, give it a shake and use ground ivy energy to "hook on to" the emotion or problem and pull it out of the body, as if pulling a piece of string.

IMPATIENS (*Impatiens glandulifera*): Instills patience and calm; understanding; knowledge that all life continues in its own unique time; development of your own deepest true timing; becoming aware of disturbances caused by others; helping to express yourself clearly toward others. Allows you to adapt easily to others without expressing irritation and annoyance. Inhibits wanting to grow too fast; being drawn too easily out of your own life's timing by the influence of others; and not expressing this and getting annoyed. Impatiens is also very helpful in cases of skin problems; in these cases impatiens can be used directly from the stock bottle.

LITTLE INKY CAP (*Coprinus xanthotrix*): When feeling vulnerable, this essence will bring emotional strength and give universal trust. Helps you rise above emotions and promotes the letting go of old anger and emotions quickly and easily. When others try to push you around or get the better of you, little inky cap helps you to remain strong and gives the ability to stand up, without hesitating, for your own viewpoints and feelings.

MONEY PLANT (*Lunaria annua*): This essence works well for those who find material, earthly business more important than unity with their own being, the universe, and nature; those who experience lack of balance in connection with spiritual development through too much striving after worldly possessions and power. Because of this tendency, these people become unable to make contact with their own source — retarding spiritual development and creating, as a result, a state of emptiness in the subconscious. They fill this emptiness with activities that seem to be forced on them from the outside but that they, in fact, draw to themselves. They feel they "have to" do so many things. When you feel you don't get enough, this essence gives faith in the abundance of the universe. It is also good for jealous children.

MOTHERWORT (*Leonurus cardiaca*): The motherwort flower essence works on and resolves old family patterns and problems, especially those related to issues of love and support. It is for those who don't feel at home in their family and on earth and easily feel under attack. If you have not received the warmth and love of family, as a result you may have become hardened and rigid, and you feel like a stranger on the earth. Just like the motherwort plant, you become prickly and start reacting negatively to those around you. When you are stiff and starchy, motherwort helps you to loosen up, transforming what has become overstructured and overorganized. It is particularly good for helping people let go of the fear of being hurt.

MYCENA (*Mycena polygramma*): This mushroom remedy is a good cleanser for deep, unresolved emotions. Improves your connection with the earth and your ability to carry on in difficult situations and amid uncertainties, especially when everything around you seems to be in ruins. At the same time, it has a purifying action and restoring effect on the aura. In nature, mushrooms help in the breaking down of hard elements that are difficult to "digest."

ORCHID (*Cephalanthera rubra*): The message of this orchid is unity of being in all circumstances. It gives inner certainty and encourages not letting yourself be pushed aside by people or circumstances but following your own path in purity. Lets the unique person that you are be seen by the outside world. Opens you to "higher" energies. Can be helpful for healers especially when there is a problem with the energy. Gives more power for the healing of others and lets this force stream out of the Higher Self into the world. Helps you to be a bearer of the Light.

PEPPERMINT (*Mentha piperita*): Peppermint helps you to digest everything that is difficult, especially what is happening in this moment in your life and in the world. It helps you deal with deep emotions and problems that you see in the world around you, all the things that come your way and that you cannot get out of your mind. Peppermint essence also gives you insight into the behavior patterns and structures you have been holding on to since the time you were born. It might even be that you are no longer aware of these patterns and structures. Peppermint gives the insight that these are a part of you and that they may be blocking the development and growth of your highest good.

PURPLE FLOWER (*Centratherum punctatum*): Brings lightness to energies around the head and brings awareness in healing. Allows the mind to relax. Allows you to reflect the light of your being into the different kingdoms (animal, mineral, plant, and human), to open up to the power of nature, and to become aware of your environment with regard to the different kingdoms.

RED HENBIT (*Lamium purpureum*): Strengthens earthly bonds and brings joy in physical activity. Gives clarity in chaotic activity, stimulating you to tidy up and put everything in order — very useful when you are moving house. Purifies your energies, providing a strong flow of earthy life force through the body, soul, and spirit, flushing away confrontational situations. Can also be applied topically for blockages in the wrists and other joints. Red henbit is a positive catalyst that promotes love for your environment and a joyful life.

RED POPPY (*Papaver rhoeas*): Strengthens the inner woman. A warming and empowering essence for those who feel vulnerable without having the power to transform their vulnerabilities. Gives you the power to work with your vulnerabilities. Strengthens the link with the feminine force and the earth. Increases the inner quality of love. Balances sexuality in men and women. Helpful also for men and children, especially when they cannot sleep after a busy day.

RUE (*Ruta graveolens*): For spiritual protection, especially in the psychic realms. Gives protection and insight when somebody is trying to absorb your energies, by spiritual influence or interference, especially in the area of the crown chakra and the line of connection with the Higher Self. Gives insights into old, deeply hidden fears. Gives more strength to act out of the feeling world. If you are overprecise, this essence helps you to see things with more ease.

SENSITIVE WEED (*Mimosa pudica*): When others come too close and you no longer have enough room, or when you are oversensitive, this essence helps you choose your path, full of certainty, and not let yourself be drawn off course. Helps you to pursue your self-development under all circumstances, to feel yourself protected and supported by your environment, and to accept this support and love. Sensitive weed has given good results with clients with high or low blood pressure.

SMOOTH HAWKSBEARD (*Crepis capillaris*): Helps to bring balance between action and repose; opens you up to new energy and vitality; and gives suppleness to stiff, rigid structures. Helps you to be at one with yourself and feel at ease and at home with others, thus helping you to clear up emotional "stuff" related to relationships in the home, from your childhood right up to today. Helps in recharging energy and in the giving of love and warmth.

SNEEZEWORT (*Achillea ptarmica*): Provides protection on the spiritual path you follow, when you aspire after pure standards and values but have been unable to actualize them. Helps you to stand on your own two feet and to give expression to your own clear thoughts and visions, without having to lean on others. Gives self-confidence. Helps to make you aware of what is good and what is not so concerning help from others (such as from spiritual guides). The essence has also given good results for sneezing problems due to cat and dog hair and dust.

SNOWDROP (*Galanthus nivalis*): Helps you to release deep pain, tears, and old traumas that have been stored up for a long time, especially when these originate from not being true to your own heart and not standing up for yourself and your feelings; when you have done everything for others and have forgotten yourself; when you do everything the way others say to, while you know that it should be done differently. Helps you to recover your own beauty and importance, to do things you like to do, to feel free. Brings a stronger trust, deep down in the depths of your being. Is joyful and refreshing after the long and dark emotional winter.

STAR OF BETHLEHEM (*Ornithogalum umbellatum*): The star of Bethlehem helps you to remain undisturbed by influences coming from your surroundings and reconnects you with your universal being. It starts by helping you clear away anything you have assimilated, especially what you have drawn to yourself that is not essential for your being. It helps you to clear away what is blocking your own unique flowering and the connection with your Higher Self, anything you have allowed in that is not a part of your original being but has accumulated throughout your life. It is a truly universal flower essence that makes you believe in your own beauty.

STROPHARIA AURANTIACA (*Redlead Roundhead*): This essence relieves sadness connected to the feeling of not belonging on earth, resulting in being unable to manifest the fire/strength of your Higher Self. Helps you to feel happy and contented, have few needs, and have confidence in the universe. Makes you aware of why you do not feel happy on earth and of the cause of your vulnerability, and enables you to let go of it through trust. Helps with the clearing of emotions originating in past sorrow, from failed relationships and failed actions to more recent provocations. Helps you to take life as it comes. Brings insight into how to handle things so that you don't fall into the same old behavior patterns. Many clients report good results in clearing up dizzy spells, as in Ménière's disease, with this essence.

SUNFLOWER (*Helianthus tuberosus*): This perennial sunflower works on the father principle, in both men and women. Helps you stand up for yourself, restores the connection with the father archetype, and helps you to release old father-related problems. Strengthens the solar plexus and helps you to find your own power. Helps you with the manifestation of your dreams. Gives strength, vitality, and energy. Gives you decisiveness and the ability to take action. Good to use for a dominating father or mother and/or an absent father or mother.

TANSY (*Tanacetum vulgare*): When you are always in doubt and cannot make decisions, tansy helps you to take direct action and gives insight; if you are not making decisions, nothing will happen. When you are caught up in a web of hesitation, tansy will give you trust and help to connect you with your Higher Self. Strengthens the heart and gives insight into the deepest core of doubts on all levels of your being.

TRUMPET VINE (*Campsis radicans*): When communication problems need solving, the trumpet vine breaks through the communication barriers in a gentle way, helping you to express your deeper emotions without being in conflict with yourself. Whenever a thick wall has been set up around somebody, the trumpet vine helps you to break this down in a very smooth and gentle way, since it first helps you to break down your own inner wall. You start doing what you really like to do, instead of what you have been conditioned to think you should be doing. It has produced good results with people who stutter.

YELLOW STAR TULIP (*Calochortus monophyllus*): This remedy helps sensitive people who are no longer sure where they are going. It helps you to not hide your sensitivity but to make use of it. It is also a precious help for bringing into being what your heart tells you and for starting on projects that have been inside you for some time but that have remained hidden deep within. Yellow star tulip gives a clearer picture of how your own feelings are put together. It gives you trust in all changes and stimulates you to act. Your inner life qualities are brought to the surface and find their outward expression both in developing the Self and in helping others.

Combination Remedies

ANIMAL FREEDOM: This combination remedy helps to free the soul of the animal. It releases animals from the problems and sufferings they have taken over from their people. Animal Freedom also releases animals from the problems and suffering inflicted on them by humans, in both a conscious and a subconscious way. Many problems for animals are related to their people's tensions and stress. This combination gives animals the feeling of freedom, making them feel calm and at ease. It connects animals to their original strength and being, so that they can live out the original purpose of their lives. This remedy has also given good results in cases of epilepsy.

CELL PHONE: This combination remedy protects against the radiation of cell phones. You can hold the essence near the phone when you are using it, or you can put a little bit of the essence on your head near where you hold the phone. When you already have a headache because of too much cell phone use, you can put a drop of this combination on the painful spot several times. It is also good for when you are hypersensitive to electricity.

4 ELEMENTS: This essence allows you to be open and warm toward others while remaining yourself. The contact with your soul and the purpose of your soul become clearer. It helps you to release what is hindering your evolution, to remain aware of your own power, and to accept others as they are. Gives you a feeling of freedom, joy, and openness because you can act with more power and self-assurance. Allows you to take over your own space and heal and nurture it from your Higher Self.

4 MUSHROOMS: The 4 Mushrooms combination helps you to express yourself in the most powerful way, for your manifestation. It also helps you to release old compromises you have made to accommodate others and removes the confusion you have taken on from them. It gives you the faith and the courage to let go, which enables you to break through old layers and patterns that would otherwise cause a blockage.

INTEGRATION: This remedy helps with integration, protection, and the resolution of old emotions that have not been processed. The Integration combination helps you to let go of the old and gives insight into how problems came about. This can be related to past relationships, past misfortunes, and abuse. It helps you to resolve all situations in which you have been hurt and offended or have lost control over your life, even sometimes just for a moment.

LIVING STAR LIGHT: This essence connects you with your natural earth being and with the stars. It instills trust, relaxes you, and releases you from everything that is not part of your being. First it helps you to find the wholeness of your being on earth, and then it deepens the connection of your being with the earth and with the cosmic energies.

LOVE: This combination awakens love for yourself, others, and the earth. It first strengthens your connection with the earth and then opens your heart for the care and love of your own being. As a result, you are able to give this love to others, without denying your own needs; you give love with pleasure from out of the source of your own self. This combination is a powerful catalyst that connects you to your Angel of Love.

PROTECTION: This combination provides protection; it surrounds you with a mantle of light and strengthens your aura. It calms you and brings you to the deepest center of your being in times of tension caused by the outer world.... An important essence when you are attacked by voodoo or negative energies, or when people are trying to absorb your energies. Strengthens your self-protection.

PURITY: This essence was first used as a combination remedy for headaches. It purifies your soul and your body and connects you to the earth. It helps you feel like you fit in your body better, and connects you to the original purity of your soul, your origin. Also helps to clear unnecessary emotions and strengthens your self-confidence.

RAINBOW: Rainbow is a bridge between heaven and earth. This combination essence is for personal development and is made from the flowers of borage, impatiens, money plant, red henbit, and red poppy. Brings creativity and development, opens you to the new, and helps you release the old. While the Terra essence (see below) helps you make the vertical connection to the earth, the Rainbow essence also works horizontally; it brings expansion and new impulses, stimulates new activities, opens all chakras, helps break barriers that block your development, and brings awareness to the process of development.

THE SPIRITUAL PATH: This combination helps you find your spiritual direction when you have made choices that were not spiritually motivated; when you have made the material world and material things most important in your life. It helps to change the choices you have made in the past and gives you the insight that there is no material world without a spiritual world.

TERRA (an emergency combination): Terra is well suited as a first-aid remedy for all different kinds of complaints. First it clears blockages and then helps with the recovery process. Brings peace and calm in tense situations. Opens the solar plexus and gives strength in difficult circumstances. A good essence for exams, journeys, work or relationship stress, illness, grief, and burnout. Also good for plants and animals. In extreme situations, it is best to take two drops under the tongue straight from the stock bottle and/or to hold the remedy bottle during prolonged periods of tension.

TERRA EXTRA (an emergency combination): A remedy for when you have used the normal Terra for a longer period than usual or when the stress and tension are due to old, deep-rooted, or very high tensions. Terra Extra gives you a stronger connection with your soul and a deeper, more refined connection with the earth, and it works harder to develop the feminine. Terra Extra draws you out of your head and brings you back into the here and now, so you remain present to yourself and release your emotions.

Essences of the New Times

ANGEL AND LEMURIAN PORTAL (with the orchid *Cephalanthera rubra*): This essence goes to the origin of who you are, beyond the limiting codes that keep you locked in old structures. Transformation takes place because you open up to the source of Higher Knowledge. When you have the feeling that you can't go on, can't take the next step, and are running around in circles, this essence opens your connection with the angelic world and aligns you with the wisdom and knowledge of Lemuria. This essence also transforms the old grief that blocks you to the new. It strengthens your connection with your angel/guidance/Higher Self so you can clearly follow your path.

CELL ENERGY: The Cell Energy essence reconnects the cells with their original structure. It brings you back to the original frequency of the cell, and it brings the inner cells of humans and animals back in harmony with their original task on earth, without having to clear all the old emotions. This essence is like a spiritual bypass; it helps you start doing what fits you, helps to remove blockages, and brings you into your power, beyond everything, back to the source. From there you recharge yourself and start finding your own way.

CORNCOCKLE (*Agrostemma githago*): This essence brings clarity and encourages you to follow the direction of your heart. It helps you to assimilate unknown chaotic emotions. Lets you make a vision quest to your center, passing by all disturbing influences. Supports you in standing strong for yourself and not giving in. It gives the insight that if you want to move on, the growth and development of consciousness are necessary. Helps you to release feelings of revenge and opens you to the higher consciousness of forgiveness and love. There is one certainty: that you are a child of God (the universe). When you have lost faith in your life, in the world, in humanity, Corncockle brings you back to a state of purity.

EARTH CREATION: This essence gives you the peace and faith to be, without struggle, to stand in your power without pain. It gives you deep roots to complete your incarnation on earth and brings humans to a new level of understanding. Initiates a cycle of healing the human race that begins with a true expression of love, the opening of the heart, and the search for real healing in yourself. Earth Creation helps you to release what is not important for fulfilling the unique role of humans in the universe and lets you descend to the earth to a level of totality, to go back from there to the level of the angels, to be healed after a long search for the original source.

EARTH PROTECTION: This is a new essence. It is made from smoky quartz, Himalaya quartz, emerald, tourmaline, labradorite, malachite, garnet, and the flower essence of motherwort, among others. The Earth Protection essence helps to protect against the physical, emotional, mental, and spiritual attacks on the energy of a person, especially the kind of draining that consists of "low" earthly energy. The flower essence Protection (see page 195) works from the spiritual and higher consciousness, the area of the crown and higher. But the Earth Protection essence strengthens the green protection and the green energy of the earth, whereby everything someone tries to do to you is reflected and you are assimilated in the protective energy of the earth.

PEAR (*Pyrus communis hybride*): This pear blossom essence gives balance and helps you stay close to yourself. It strengthens your inner power and security. It gives you trust in your inner world so you can release the things in the outside world that you put too much trust in. Pear also gives you the insight that the way you think about persons and situations doesn't always have to be true. You can also take Pear during pregnancy, when you get out of balance because of all the changes in your body. Pear also connects you with the earth when the frequency of the universe rises, so you keep the balance between below and above, matter and spirit, earth and heaven. Pear feeds you and strengthens your love for yourself. It opens you to the new and gives you insight into how to manifest yourself.

ROUND-LEAFED WINTERGREEN (*Pyrola rotundifolia*): This flower essence helps you digest nutrition from the earth, and it keeps you going while you drop everything that does not belong to you. Wintergreen gives you self-confidence and makes you aware of the fact that you have many more qualities in you than you show. It puts you in your own power, and because of this you can release old, unprocessed emotions. It lets you move on and helps you to expand and have faith in yourself, so that you can bring out the qualities that you have hidden deep inside.

Notes

Introduction

1. For more about clicker training, visit Karen Pryor's website; she is the originator of the technique: www.clickertraining.com. TTouch is a style of bodywork for animals developed by Linda Tellington-Jones and based on the Feldenkrais bodywork method for humans; for more, visit www.ttouch.com.

Chapter 1: Through the Animal Looking Glass

1. Here is the link for "A Doggy Christmas Surprise": http://www.you tube.com/watch?v=AUtPKbMwnR0&feature=player_embedded.
2. For an interview with one of the Hungarian trainers, see Lisa Wogan, "The Mirror Method," *The Bark*, no. 62 (November/December 2010), http://www.thebark.com/content/mirror-method.
3. *Schutzhund* is a German word meaning "protection dog." It refers to a sport that includes tracking, obedience, and protection work.
4. See the website for the film *Buck*, www.buckthefilm.com, where this quote comes from. For an interesting interview with Brannaman in connection with the movie, visit: http://blog.beliefnet.com/movie mom/2011/06/interview-buck-brannaman-the-real-horse-whisperer .html#ixzz25eLFsPXz.

5. Shakti Gawain, *Living in the Light* (Novato, CA: New World Library, 2011).

6. Carol Gurney is a world-renowned animal communicator and founder of the Gurney Institute of Animal Communication. To learn more, visit her website at www.gurneyinstitute.com.

7. Fracking is short for hydraulic fracturing. It's an extremely water-intensive process where millions of gallons of fluid — typically a mix of water, sand, and chemicals, including ones known to cause cancer — are injected underground at high pressure to fracture the rock surrounding an oil or gas well. This fracking releases extra oil and/or gas from the rock, so it can flow into the well. It is also damaging underground water sources and is facing growing opposition.

8. To learn more about Tina Hutton, visit her website at http://tina hutton.com. CMT stands for certified massage therapist.

9. Quote from author interview with Tina Hutton, August 4, 2012.

10. For more information on Turid Rugaas, see www.canis.no/rugaas; for Michael Grant White, see www.breathing.com; and for TTEAM, www.ttouch.com/whyTTEAM.shtml.

11. To see Yuri Shimojo's work, in particular her pieces about the situation in Japan, visit her website, www.yurishimojo.com.

12. Margot Lasher, *And the Animals Will Teach You: Discovering Ourselves through Our Relationships with Animals* (New York: Berkeley Books, 1996); Margot Lasher, *Dog Pure Awareness* (Kingsport, TN: Twilight Times Books, 2008).

13. Quotes from author interview with Beverley Kane, July 4, 2012. To learn more about Dr. Kane's work, visit her website, www.horsensei.com.

Chapter 2: Our Animals, Ourselves

1. Dianne Skafte, *When Oracles Speak: Understanding the Signs and Symbols All Around Us* (Wheaton, IL: Quest Books, 2000).

2. For a description of Janis Dickinson's work, see John Roach, "Biologists Study Evolution of Animal Cooperation," *National Geographic News* (July 9, 2003), http://news.nationalgeographic .com/news/2003/07/0709_030709_socialanimals.html.

3. Rupert Sheldrake, *Science Set Free: 10 Paths to New Discovery* (New York: Deepak Chopra Books, 2012).

4. Edward O. Wilson, *Sociobiology* (Cambridge, MA: Harvard University Press, 1975).

5. For Ginny's story, along with those of other dog heroes, see the Dog Guide website, "25 Heroic Dogs and How They Saved People," http://www.dogguide.net/25-hero-dogs.php/.

6. Jeffrey Masson and Susan McCarthy, *When Elephants Weep: The Emotional Lives of Animals* (New York: Bantam Doubleday Dell Publishing Group, 1995); Marc Bekoff, *The Emotional Lives of Animals: A Leading Scientist Explores Animal Joy, Sorrow, and Empathy — And Why They Matter* (Novato, CA: New World Library, 2007).

7. Electa Draper, "Canine Emotions Raise Theological Questions," *Denver Post*, May 16, 2009, http://www.denverpost.com/ci_12382762 #ixzz26WhxCYJY.

8. For an overview of animal intelligence evidence and research, see "NOVA: How Smart Are Animals," PBS (February 9, 2011), http://www.pbs.org/wgbh/nova/nature/how-smart-are-animals.html. See also the animal intelligence blog page by Christiane Bailey, http://christianebailey.com/animal-intelligence-podcast/.

9. Bekoff quote from Draper, "Canine Emotions Raise Theological Questions," http://www.denverpost.com/ci_12382762#ixzz26 WhxCYJY.

10. Lasher, *And the Animals Will Teach You*, 212.

11. For more on this movie, visit the website www.horseboymovie.com.

12. Lasher, *And the Animals Will Teach You*, 230–31.

Chapter 3: Positive Mirroring

1. To learn more about Dr. Maryanne Kraft, visit her website, http://drkraft.net.

2. To learn more about Carol Gurney, visit her website, www.gurney institute.com.

3. To learn more about Carol Upton, visit her website, www.dreams aloud.ca. This story can be found at http://cf4aass.org/_archives /CarolUptonHealingwithAnimalsStory.pdf.

4. Melanie LaCour, "TRF: From Prison to Paddock," *Florida Horse* 55, no. 6 (August 2012): 50–54, http://issuu.com/floridahorse/docs/august 2012binder?mode=window&viewMode=doublePage.

Chapter 4: Negative Mirroring

1. At this stage in my life with animals, I have chosen to work with holistic vets to devise the care I give my animals. I no longer use pesticides for parasite control, and I avoid vaccines when possible, as I have seen my animals have adverse reactions to chemicals and vaccines. I also try to avoid drugs and use alternatives like herbs, homeopathics, acupuncture, bodywork, and chiropractic to help my animals when they are ill. In addition, I only feed my animals whole, real, organic food. There have been so many recalls I just find it hard to trust commercial food anymore. Plus even the best commercial food, even when organic, is no better than if we ate tinned meat and veggies and dry cereal all the time. To learn more, check out the resources and books on my website, http://martawilliams.com.

2. To learn more about Su Wickersham, visit her blog, http://doglisten .wordpress.com.

3. To see Joni McKim's art, visit her website, http://jonimckim.com.

4. To learn about Kati Gabor's work, visit her website, www.earth connections.ca.

5. Visit Gene Leon and Kinna Ohman's blog at www.backtoearth friends.org.

6. Here are two books on reincarnation to start with: Brian Weiss, *Many Lives, Many Masters: The True Story of a Prominent Psychiatrist, His Young Patient, and the Past-Life Therapy That Changed Both Their Lives* (New York: Fireside, 1988), and Gary Schwartz, *The Afterlife Experiments: Breakthrough Scientific Evidence of Life after Death* (New York: Pocket Books, 2002).

Chapter 5: In Sickness and in Health

1. While a lot of holistic health care resources are listed in this chapter, see my website for more: http://martawilliams.com.

2. Martin Goldstein, *The Nature of Animal Healing: The Definitive Holistic Medicine Guide to Caring for Your Dog and Cat* (New York: Ballantine Books, 2000).

3. To learn more about Dr. Ian Billinghurst, visit his website, www.barfaustralia.com.

4. Learn more about why commercial food is not good for your

animals, read "What's Really in Pet Food," on Born Free USA, http://www.bornfreeusa.org/facts.php?more=1&p=359.

5. In addition to visiting my website, here are some other resources for holistic horse care. For advice on safely feeding and grazing horses, visit http://safergrass.org. For holistic advice on vaccines, visit http://www.holistichorsekeeping.com/resources/articles /vaccinations.html. When it comes to tack, I prefer a bitless bridle and a treeless saddle.

6. To learn more about enteroliths, see the web page http://evrp.lsu .edu/healthtips/Enteroliths-Colic.htm.

7. Herb Tanzer, *Your Pet Isn't Sick, He Just Wants You to Think So* (Philadelphia: Wharton Publishing, 1998).

8. To learn more about holistic veterinary medicine, see Lisa Pesch's website, www.healingpetsnaturally.com.

9. Louise Hay, *Heal Your Body* (Carlsbad, CA: Hay House, 1984).

10. To learn more about Julie Motz, visit her website, http://juliemotz.com.

Chapter 6: Look in the Mirror — What Do You See?

1. Pete Sanders, *You Are Psychic!* (New York: Fawcett Columbine Books, 1989).

2. See Hay, *Heal Your Body*; Bram Zaalberg, *Spiegel je met bloesem-remedies* (The Netherlands: Ankh-Hermes, 2002); and Ryke Geerd Hamer's website, www.newmedicine.ca. Other sources include www.paganspath.com, http://www.speedyremedies.com /metaphysical-causes-of-disease.html, and http://www.articlesbase .com/cancer-articles/emotional-causes-of-cancer-negative-emotions -in-the-body-can-cause-cancer-very-interesting-article-906066.html.

3. To learn about Carolyn Resnick's unique ground-training techniques for horses, visit her website, www.carolynresnickblog.com.

Chapter 7: Cleaning the Mirror

1. Louise Hay, *You Can Heal Your Life* (Carlsbad, CA: Hay House, 1984/2006), 76.

2. Some of my favorites books about manifesting are Michael Losier, *Law of Attraction* (Victoria, BC, Canada: Michael J. Losier Enterprises, 2006), and Denise Coates, *Feel It Real!* (New York: Atria Books, 2008).

3. Hay, *You Can Heal Your Life*, 84.
4. To learn more about shamanic journeying, visit the website www.shamanism.org.

Conclusion: Mirror, Mirror, Everywhere

1. Richard Louv, *Last Child in the Woods* (Chapel Hill, NC: Algonquin Books, 2008).

Appendix: Dutch Flower Essence Remedies

1. The flower essence material, and the specific remedy descriptions, in this appendix are taken from Bram Zaalberg, *Spiegel je met bloesem-remedies* (The Netherlands: Ankh-Hermes, 2002), and the website www.bloesem-remedies.com/english.

Index

About the Author

Biologist Marta Williams now works full-time as an animal communicator. She has authored three previous books, published by New World Library, on the subject of animal communication: *Ask Your Animal*, *Beyond Words*, and *Learning Their Language*. Marta lives in Northern California, teaches worldwide and by teleclass, and offers consultations for animals and their people by phone, Skype, and email. Visit her website at www.martawilliams.com and her blog at www.martawilliamsblog.com

NEW WORLD LIBRARY is dedicated to publishing books and other media that inspire and challenge us to improve the quality of our lives and the world.

We are a socially and environmentally aware company, and we strive to embody the ideals presented in our publications. We recognize that we have an ethical responsibility to our customers, our staff members, and our planet.

We serve our customers by creating the finest publications possible on personal growth, creativity, spirituality, wellness, and other areas of emerging importance. We serve New World Library employees with generous benefits, significant profit sharing, and constant encouragement to pursue their most expansive dreams.

As a member of the Green Press Initiative, we print an increasing number of books with soy-based ink on 100 percent postconsumer-waste recycled paper. Also, we power our offices with solar energy and contribute to nonprofit organizations working to make the world a better place for us all.

Our products are available
in bookstores everywhere.
For our catalog, please contact:

New World Library
14 Pamaron Way
Novato, California 94949

Phone: 415-884-2100 or 800-972-6657
Catalog requests: Ext. 50
Orders: Ext. 52
Fax: 415-884-2199
Email: escort@newworldlibrary.com

To subscribe to our electronic newsletter, visit:
www.newworldlibrary.com

HELPING TO PRESERVE OUR ENVIRONMENT

3,147 trees were saved

New World Library uses 100% postconsumer-waste recycled paper for our books whenever possible, even if it costs more. During 2011 this choice saved the following precious resources:

www.newworldlibrary.com

ENERGY	WASTEWATER	GREENHOUSE GASES	SOLID WASTE
22 MILLION BTU	600,000 GAL.	770,000 LB.	225,000 LB.

Environmental impact estimates were made using the Environmental Defense Fund Paper Calculator @ www.papercalculator.org.